PYTHON FOR

ANALYSIS

A Beginner's Guide to Wrangling
and Analyzing Data Using Python

Clark Wes

indirect, which are incurred as a result of the use of information contained within this document, including, but not limited to, — errors, omissions, or inaccuracies.

INTRODUCTION

Python programming has brought revolutionary strides in the data management industry. Data is very sensitive, and thus there needs to be an accurate way of relaying information with utmost accuracy. That is where Python programming comes in; to bring revolution and provide users with accurate results.

This book enlightens the readers on the basics of Python programming. It also provides the details that all beginners should know about when venturing into the programming world. By the end of reading this book, you should be well equipped with the necessary tools and skills to conquer the programming industry.

Much effort was made to ensure that the readers get the most accurate information. Every little detail of this book has been well-researched to provide readers with truthful information. Also, the report found in this book is a reflection of what most programmers go through when developing problem-solving programs.

Please enjoy!

... to all the people who didn't believe in me ...

Contents

CHAPTER 1

INTRODUCTION OF PYTHON FOR DATA ANALYSIS

Python is among the most popular computer language programming tool initially created and designed by Guido Van Rossum in the late 1980s. Since its introduction into the computing world, Python has undergone multiple modifications and improvements, therefore, becoming among leading programming languages used by developers. The tool is dynamically typed, object-oriented, multi-paradigm, and imperative. It is used across different operating systems including Windows, Linux, Android, macOS, and iOS devices. Besides, it is compatible with both bit 32 and bit 64 gadgets of phones, laptops, and desktops.

Despite comprising of several areas essential for programmers, Python is easy to learn, especially when it comes to beginners with minimal knowledge in computer programming. Unlike most programming languages, Python accompanies an easy to use syntaxes where first time users can readily practice and become a pro within a few weeks. However, the programming processes may vary depending on the motive of the learner in programming. Despite accompanying multiple vocabularies and sometimes sophisticated tutorials for learning different programming techniques, engaging with Python is worth it to develop excellent programs.

Features of Python Programming

Simple Language

Most programming languages have complicated and lengthy coding languages which may become cumbersome to beginners. More so, long and challenging languages may become hard to learn and remember, therefore hindering amateurs learning abilities. As mentioned, Python accompanies very simple and fantastic syntax, making beginners read and write programs without complications readily. When compared to Java and C++, Python henceforth enables you to work with ease while focusing on the outcomes.

Portability

With its ability to run in any operating system, Python allows for portability where you can readily transfer your codes and the general program from one device to the other without affecting your progress. This programming tool is quite useful for developers who change devices or transfer data from one platform to the other. You can, therefore, run your program in the new machine seamlessly with limited alliteration. Besides, Python allows the continuation of your application to your primary system and run effectively as intended.

Standard Libraries

Today, all programming languages consists of libraries where you can quickly select a program, make modifications are necessary, and execute your codes. Some of these libraries may have limited coding lines which will, therefore, require you to write your program. Python, on the other hand, comes with an extensive standard library which comprises of all your programming needs. For example, it consists of the MySQLdb library, which allows you to connect to the MySQL database without creating a pathway. As such, Python becomes among the leading programming tools to be used commercially when dealing with thousands of data as you can quickly retrieve and run with ease.

Free Open-Sources

Python also offers a fantastic free and open-source where you can use the tool in different areas, for example, in commercial use. Unlike other programming tools, a developer can choose to make changes on the program or instead select the desirable dataset to suit the field at hand mainly in the Python source code. While being used across several areas in the computing community, Python has experienced a constant increase in the usage, therefore, becoming more simple benefitting beginners significantly.

Downloading and Installing Python

Python, like most computer software, can be downloaded, run, and installed in a system for it to function with ease. However, this tool may become a bit challenging during download or updating, depending on the operating system. Some systems such as macOS and Linux typically accompany a preinstalled Python version which mostly is outdated. These versions of Python will hence require an update which usually uses unique techniques. On the contrary, other operating systems such as Windows and Android devices require a user to visit Python homepage or other relevant websites, download and install the software.

Python Development and Application

Python development is usually undertaken by the Python Enhancement Proposal (PEP), which has led to the creation of the most advanced and latest version. PEP has enhanced the features, Python documentation as well as the creation of bug fixes essential for eliminating problems arising during programming. Besides, it has managed to design modern coding processes as well as extending standard libraries to suit all developer needs during the creation of programs. In most cases, PEP collects information from developers utilizing Python and develops solutions on major problems raised.

When Python was first released in the 1980s, it accompanied multiple benefits but with numerous faults within the tool. Over the years, the Python Software Foundation has made significant modifications indicating differences between Python 1.0 and Python 3.7 used today. Python has henceforth gained popularity over time and applied in various areas in the computing community. For instances, the programming software has been used in the creation of Web apps in different websites such as Instagram, Mozilla, and Reddit. Other applications include the computation of both scientific and numerical values and the development of software prototype. Due to it's easy to use language, Python is widely used in educating children and beginners interested in learning computer language skills.

Python Variables

Python variables are named sections used to store codes in the system memory used mainly for the development of programs. Variables are critical in Python, especially for programmers who create complex programs in need of multiple code values. Unlike other programming software like Java and C++, Python doesn't demand variable declaration as they instantly change after being named. Python variables, therefore, are memory reserves used to store values fed to the program when needed. The data saved usually vary depending on the data type; for instance, they may be stored in the form of Numbers, Lists, Tuple, or as Dictionary.

Lists include ordered and changeable data written in the form of "my computer" with double-quotes. You can access values within the list using index numbers which are written up to negative integers. Dictionaries entail indexed and changeable variables but remain unordered and written with single curly quotes. Accessing values in dictionaries consist of inputting a keyword in parentheses which also helps in other functions such as looping, making changes, and more. Numbers are of three forms int, float and complex representing different number value stored while tuple is data values which are ordered but remain unchangeable.

Naming Variables in Python

The naming of variables, especially in Python is useful as it makes these storage units to be easily identified by a different programmer. Naming is smooth, unlike other programming tools as beginners can also assign a name to a given variable. However, assigning titles in any computer language programming process follows specific rules to ensure the names are practical and easily recognized. This is because some names may lack a desirable representation of what is included in a given variable, thus causing confusions between programmers. Some of these rules are;

- Titles must be of singles words with no spaces between letters or numerical

- First characters must never be a number

- Never use of reserved words as variable names

- The name must consist solely of letters and numbers with underscores acting as spacers

- The name must begin with a lowercase letter

In case you assign names which do not follow these rules, the system will reject the name as it is cases sensitive. Customarily, the system may act as a guide when naming your variable as it readily notifies you where the mistake has been made. There are some situations where a developer may choose to assign multiple names towards one variable. That is, writing two or more words to describe what is included in the variable. In this case, you are eligible to create your name but following either one of the methods used.

The Pascal case method is one of the ways you can use as it involves the first and subsequent words to be capitalized for readability enhancement. An example of Pascal case is PythonProgrammingLangauge. Another method is the Camel case and is where the second and subsequent words are capitalized. An example is pythonProgrammingLangauage. Lastly, Snake case is another method, and this uses underscores as spacers when creating your variable name. For instance, python_Programming_Language. All the three modes of multi-name given to Python variables are correct, and you can choose from while assigning your variable a title.

Types of Data Variables

Int

This is a number data variable stored in 16-bit values and range between -32,768 and 32,767 in Python but depends in regard to other programming tools. int stores up to 2's complement math which suggests that it can provide reserves for negative numbers. Therefore, int has a higher probability of providing adequate storage units of quite smaller amounts. When dealing with arithmetic variables, then int plays a significant role in feeding your program with the intended data.

Char

Char are data variables used to store data codes expressed in literal values and written with single quotes such as 'A.' The values are also numerical but with direct visibility to the codes used in a given program. Char, therefore, make the performance of arithmetic functions quite useful as the data is usually stored in 8-bit but those with higher memory usage being stored in bytes. Chars are typically the smaller storage units of bytes.

Bytes

Bytes are much higher data storage units essential for storing values with higher memory usage and those which cannot be stored in chars. More so, bytes are also used in the storage of 8-bit unsigned numbers which are from 0-255. Bytes and chars play a similar role as data type storage reserves of numbers but vary when it comes to the size of values stored in each section.

Strings

This is another form of a data variable which creates a series of char data types or data stored in the form of a chain. The syntax used has several declarations before the values are marked for use as strings comprise of arrays of chars. Strings are typically showed with double quotes and may store a large number of values within one chain. More so, the chars can also be broken down to form other chains as though would require many declarations when retrieving the needed data to create a program.

Python Debugging

Debugging is the process or technique used to detect and eliminate problems which arise during writing and execution of a program. Since its incorporation in the 1940s, computer debugging has become one of the techniques used to prevent errors, bugs as well as mistakes arising during programming processes. The direct opposite of the term is anti-debugging which entail reversing the method of detecting and removing such errors with tools such as modified codes, API-based and timing and latency.

In Python, the software also includes debugging but primarily depends on Python interpreter to reading recognize and eliminate problems. In some cases, Python debugging is quite effective and enables programmers to engage in the creation of programs after every breakpoint. When writing codes, you may continually input your codes without recognizing errors, bugs, or even typos may affect your outcome. Therefore, debuggers tend to indicate these problems and may either provide solutions instantly or take a breaking point for you to correct it.

Process of Computer Debugging

Problems Identification and Reproduction

When writing codes, you begin writing from the command line and you may either write continuously or the computer executing each command when a line is done. In this case, you may run into errors, and the debuggers are hence helpful. In this step, debuggers tend to recognize these mistakes and reproduce the problem to identify its viability. Either nontrivial or other bugs can be readily identified and later replicated to ascertain how they work and affect your coding processes.

Problem Generalization

Immediately your debugger has identified and determined that the problem is unnecessary in the program, it is then simplified by breaking the bug down for an effective elimination process. The benefit of breaking down this information is it ensures that your program does not crash when parsing or affecting other health values in the program. Breaking down of these files affected enhances reproduction and subdivision of these bugs to ensure the problem is recognized easily. When these problems are generalized, you can now check them, including the source files if they have errors and need immediate action to eliminate these problems.

Removal of the Problem

The next step is to eliminate the problem using a debugger tool after a successful reproduction and simplification of the errors. The tool will scan your values, including the provision of a complete analysis of your files suspected to cause the problem. Removing the issue at the point of origin is essential as it enables you to quickly realize the source files and manage or eliminate them to avoid future occurrences of these problems. In Python, recognizing and removing coding questions usually promotes the execution of high-performance programs.

Python Debugging Tools

There are several tools used today in Python for debugging and may be confused with others therefore essential to learn about them. The tools may, however, differ in functioning depending on the operating system you have or the level of errors available in the program. Some people may tend to have more than one debugging tool with an objective of completely doing away with problems when creating their desirable programs.

Debuggers

Debugger tools, especially for Python, exist in two forms, specific tools, and multipurpose tools, depending on the program length and operating system. Some of the all-purpose debugger tools include PdbRcldea and pdb, and versatile tools include trepan2, epdb, and Winpdb, which primarily focus on the errors originating from different areas. On the other hand, specific debugger tools include DDD, Xpdb, and gdb, which identify and eliminate mistakes from particular regions. As mentioned, these debugger tools work in different areas which may include during variable naming, program creation, execution, or when writing codes.

Integrated Development Environment (IDEs)

This is one of the most used debugging tools preferably used in advanced and large projects by experienced developers. The IDEs Python debugging tools may vary of the functionality, but features accompanied usually remain the same. They also identify and eliminate programming errors on different sections, including when running your codes, evaluating variables, and designing breakpoints. The PyCharm is the commonly used debugging tool type of IDEs consisting of all the components such as plugs to maximize problem identification, simplification, and elimination.

Special-Purpose

This is another type of Python debugging tool suitable for detecting and eliminating bugs situated in the remote sections of the program. They are essential in tracing flaws and mistakes created in sensitive areas where other debugging tools are unable to detect. Some of them include FirePython used in Firefox in performing deep scans to remove hidden errors. This is one of the vital Python debugging tools which ensure that programmers do not get stuck because of mistakes originating from unknown locations within the program. As such, special-purpose debugging tools provide a conducive working environment for programmers to create applications without facing challenges arising from inconspicuous areas.

Python Compilers

A compiler is a computing term used to describe how a computer program can be translated despite being written in a specific programming language. It means that a given computer program can be converted into a simplified and readily executable program. In Python, compilers simply mean the conversion of a high-level computer language into a low-level computer language. Python typically buses Python interpreter instead of compilers to translate these complex languages. However, programmers, especially beginners, may adopt Python compilers as a substitute tool to simplify these languages.

As such, Python compilers may come in two forms; static and dynamic or used together and also used in Java. Jython is one of the commonly used Python compilers which readily translates programming language between the two platforms. Despite Python utilizing an interpreter to perform this function, it is necessary to have a compiler as Java and other programming software such as C++ lack an interpreter. Python interpreters are more flexible and beneficial, mainly when translating human language into computer language.

Types of Python Compilers

Nuitka

This is one of Python compilers which is source to source and translates Python code values to C/C++ as standalone executable programs. Nuitka solely writes in Python language while using multiple libraries and modules mostly utilized by developers in the computing world. This type of compiler is available for Windows, macOS, Linux, and FreeBSD as well as supports the functions of Anaconda.

Brython

Brython is the most commonly used Python compiler usually recognized as 'Python 3 implementation of client-side web programming'. It is one of the best compilers in the conversion of Python languages into readable Java codes. Besides, Brython can be used in the HTML5 platforms as it comes with DOM features in its package. It is also faster when compared to other compilers such as Skulpt and CPython. Features of Brython enhance its functions, making it suitable for the development of straightforward and small projects and works best with Firefox as well as other browsers.

WinPython

WinPython is designed primarily for Windows operating system devices and works as the replacement of the previous version of CPython which accompanied multiple bugs. However, the current version of CPython is quite useful for the previous one. WinPython is packed with a full library of data science and machine learning courses becoming among the self-service Python compilers today. Some of the standard libraries you will find in this compiler are SciPy, and Numpy accessed easily when in need of using them. You can readily download WinPython is your Windows operating system through the installer where you will run it will integrate with your system.

Shed Skin

Shed Skin is commonly used for between Python 2.4 and Python 2.6 as a compiler for translating static types python language to C++. It means that Shed Skin converts datatypes with single values under given specific parameters set. Despite lacking the essential features like that of other Python compilers, it accompanies excellent standard libraries making it among the most useful language translators today. On the contrary, Shed Skin may translate programs with limitations as well as unable to scale multiple line codes like most compilers. In this case, you are required to mount these lines manually, thus having exceptional standalone programs at the end.

CHAPTER 2

PYTHON PROGRAMMING IN DETAILS

Computers work by a set of instructions which are written by human beings. The set of instructions are referred to as programming. Computer programming is, therefore, a set of instructions a machine is supposed to execute. The two core elements of programming are data and interpretation of instructions. When writing computer instructions, various kinds of languages are used. These are referred to computer programming languages. This article explores some of the computer languages, history of python programming, application of python programming, and how you can download and install it.

Computer programming languages

Computers work by instructions that human beings give them. Various languages are used to offer these instructions. These are referred to computer programming languages. The part of a language the machines understand is referred to as binary. Therefore programming languages must be converted into binary for the computer to understand them. The process of translating computer language into binary is referred to as compiling. There are various computer programming languages with various unique attributes, even though most of them have some similarities. This section explores some of the computer programming languages as follows:

1. **Java**-This is data-oriented language and has a range of functions. It has various qualities, including that makes it the best for web designing and building. Programming engineers and java designers majorly use Java. Additionally, this language can be utilized by various people in communication, retailing, fiancé and education. Java is a crucial programming language because it applied in the development of business-oriented applications, computer game development and mobile apps. The core qualities of java language include high-level explainable language, robust network and easily applied.

2. **Ruby**- This language is data-oriented, publicly accessible for use and modification and can be applied alone or form part of rails web structure. This language is majorly applied by Ruby designers, programming engineers and information science professionals. It can also be utilized by various employers such as those in technology, engineering and design. The leading organizations that are applying Ruby include Blue Sequence, Google, NASA and others.

3. **HTML (HyperText Markup language)** – This language is used to form platform pages because it ensures appropriate formatting of words and photos. Various professionals can use HTML. These include platform designers, specialized editors, programming engineers

and others. Examples of employers using this language include IT engineers, Sales, and Client service. The main features of this programming language are that it's readily accessible, simple in application and exist in many versions.

4. **JavaScript**- Although this programming language sounds like Java, it isn't part of it. It's a majorly client-oriented language which operates in a customer's browser and executes instructions on a machine as opposed to a server. There are various professionals who can utilize JavaScript. These include JavaScript designers, programming engineering and others. Employers who can utilize this language include those in Finance, Healthcare and IT. The essential businesses that have utilized JavaScript include WordPress, LinkIn, and Yahoo and others. The language is simple to learn and has many structures.

5. **C Language**-This language can be used for different purposes. The language is computer independent and is majorly used in operating systems. There are various fields where this language can be used. These include software engineering, computer engineering and web content development. The significant features of this language are that include easy to master and simple to write system instructions.

Python Programming and its History

Python programming is a general-purpose language that can be applied in many fields. The program is easily accessible and resourceful in resolving many computer issues. Additionally, Python can be applied to all major computer operating systems. The language is helpful in different roles such as processing of texts and images. There are various fields where Python has been applied. These include Google, YouTube, NASA and others. A significant feature of Python is that it's an explainable language meaning that you need not transform it into machine-readable code. Although in the past, interpreted programmes have been looked down upon as inferior, Python has changed this view because vast applications are now written on it.

History of Python Programming

The history of Python is traced back to 1980s. The idea was conceived by Guido Van Rossum and designed by the Python Software Foundation. The idea was to create a programming language that resembles ABC programming. Just like the ABC programming language, the Python language was also conceived in the Netherlands. The researchers of Python language wanted to create a programming language that focuses on scanning a code and syntax that lets programers articulate ideas in minimal code lines.

Guido Van Rossum started working on the Python project in the late 1980s. For Guido van Rossum, this was a pastime idea that he was trying to see how whether it would resemble ABC programming which he played a significant role in creating. The ABC language could interface with the Amoeba operating system. Because he had worked on the ABC language, Guido Van Rossum had noted some weaknesses that he wanted to improve through Python Programming. He borrowed some notable aspects of ABC and applied them in coming up with an improved scripting language Guido Van Rossum, named this programming Python which he derived from a BBC show where he was a fan. The show was called 'Monty Python's Flying Circus.' The Python Programming language was launched in 1991. Its codes are few in comparison with C++ and C.

Python Versions

From the time of its creation, Python has had different versions. These include:

1. **Python Version 0.9.0**-This was the first version which was released in 1991 by Guido Van Rossum. The core features of this version were inheritance classes, functions, unique handling and othrs . Present in this version was a module system. There was the formation of a discussion forum for Python at this stage.

2. **Version 1**-This milestone was attained in 1994. The version had a variety of features including reduce, filter, map and others.

3. **Version 1.2**-This was released in 1995.

4. **Python 3.7.3**-This is the latest version released in 2019. It has various highlights, including context variables, classes of data, built-in breakpoints, and others. These features help the version to perform robustly and doing away with the use of ASCII

Advantages of using Python Programming language

There are various benefits of applying Python as a Programming language. These include:

1. **Variety of support libraries**-Python contains vast support libraries in various sections. These include string website, platform service equipment, and string running. The lengths of the codes are short as most programming tasks are scripted.

2. **Integration of features**-Python has certain features that make ideal for the development of web services. It applies the features of COBRA and COM to develop platform solutions. It applies various programming service like C, C++ to offer the best service.

3. **Enhances programmer's Productivity**-Due to the presence of vast support libraries, Python enhances the productivity of any programmer by enabling to apply various languages like C++ and Java.

4. **Productivity**-The Python language has robust features, testing frameworks and improved control capacities. These attributes make it enhance the speed of most of its applications.

Downsides of using Python Programming language

In spite of the various strengths of this programming language, it has various weaknesses. These include:

1. **Challenge is applying other languages**-Most Python programmers are obsessed with its features and may not learn about the other programming languages such as Java.

2. **Speed**-Because Python is an interpreted language; it's sluggish when compared to languages like C and C++. This limitation makes it not to be liked by many programmers who are conscious of the speed to execute their projects.

3. **Mobile development**-This language is not the best for mobile development. It's majorly applied on desktops and server sites.

4. **Memory application**-Python consumes enormous amounts of memory. In case you want to perform a memory-intensive exercise, it's not the best program to utilize.

5. **Run time errors**-Because python language is typed, and it has numerous model limitations. Even when you take time to test its application, still errors crop up

Applications of python programming

Due to its various features and library support system, Python has a multiplicity of applications. This section highlights and explains some of the applications as follows:

1. **Applications**-Python is applied in designing of various applications such as web, software design, Graphic design applications, scientific application and others. This is because language is friendly and highly interactive. When you apply Python, you easily develop your website with minimal trouble. The language contains libraries and tools that you can easily apply in web development. These include HTML and XML.

2. **Various programming applications**- The language is helpful to other programming languages and paradigms.

The python features help in the development of various applications which may be simple or complex.

3. **Lively library**-The robustness of python library helps programmers in developing various applications. The library helps the developer to choose Python instead of other programs whose libraries are weak. The various modules that are found within the python library assist the developer to create various functionalities.

4. **Compatibility with multiple platforms**-Python is compatible with various platforms and systems and can be applied when developing applications on them. Because the language is interpreted, it can be run on any platform and system.

5. **Access of database**-With python, you quickly access any database. Furthermore, the language can assist in individualizing the interfaces for easy application. You can access such a database like ODBC, MySQL and Oracle.

6. **Code readability**-one of the benefits of using Python is the ability to read and service the code efficiently. You can reapply the code any time the need arises — the code assists in creating personalized applications and software. Software engineers can use Python to support them when developing programs.

7. **Development of software is simplified**-When you apply Python, you simplify the process of complicated software development. You can design complicated applications like those in the areas of science and statistics. In statistics, Python can assist in areas like data analysis and visualization.

8. **An open-source framework**-Because python is an open-source computer programming language, and you can easily access it. This is important when you want to reduce the cost of software development. The many tools and libraries of Python assist you to develop your software without incurring much cost.

9. **Application of Python in desktop GUI**-Python is compatible with various features of a desktop application, including TK.

10. **Education-**Python has a large community and is one of the best programming languages that can be used at the introductory level of computer programming at schools and colleges.

11. **Python application in business-** There are various business applications which can use Python. These include Enterprise Resource Planning and online businesses.

12. Games and 3D Graphics-Pythons has features that can assist you to develop games and 3D libraries.

How Python compare to other languages

Python is one of the interpreted computer languages. Other computer programming languages that feature under this category include Java, JavaScript, Perl, and TCL. When you compare it with Java, Python is a bit slower. The python language almost works at the same level as JavaScript, although the former supports a style that applies simple functions. Python and Perl have so many things in common, although their application philosophies are different. Whereas Perl focuses support for standard applications, Python's primary concentration is support for common computer languages.

How to download and install Python

The procedure of downloading and installing Python on your machine is simple. Follow the following procedure when downloading Python:

1. Ensure that you have on your machine

2. Enter the word Python in a search engine

3. On your windows try to search for Python launcher and download the latest version of Python

The python version you install depends on the type of windows you're using. For instance, if you're operating Mac, you can install the latest version

Python is arguably one of the best computer programming languages at the moment. It has excellent features, tools and libraries that can support a multiplicity of applications. This blog has offered you helpful information about its history, applications, advantages and downloading and installing it.

CHAPTER 3

PYTHON DEBUGGING

Most programming languages do utilize debugging in order to produce unique computing programs. Python being a programming language is not exceptional.

Python debugger enables the programmer to run an application within a particular set with different breakpoints. Equally, the software provides interactive source code with a purpose of supporting under program controls. There are other actions that of Python debugger which include testing of units and integration, analysis of log files and flow, and system-level monitoring.

Depending on the provided command line and IDE system, a program can be run in the debugger with several working tools. For example, developed a more complicated and specialized computer program has lead to the expansion of debugging tools. The tools use different features to assist in detecting any abnormality, examining the impact, and planning for updates and patches to correct emerging problems. In some situations debugging tools can improve programmer's capability in the development of new programs by removing code and Unicode errors.

Debugging

Debugging is a method of testing and providing solutions for errors which may be caused by difficulties or malfunctions in a specified computer program. Admiral Grace Hopper, who was working on mark ll computers at Harvard University during the 1940s, was the first to use the name, "debugging." She realized that a number of moths within the relays were affecting computer operations hence called them "debugging" in the system. Even though the term had been earlier used by Thomas Edison in the year 1878, it became known in the 1950s when programmers started using it to refer to computer programs.

During the 1960s, computer users commonly used the term 'debugging' to explain the proposed solution to great computing difficulties; hence, it became widely known. Debugging has taken an essential scope in a world which is getting more digitalized and more challenging programs coming up — therefore removing words like computer errors, bugs, and malfunctions to a better equal position such as computer anomaly and discrepancy. However, non-aligned words are subjected to evaluation to tell whether their meanings to computing problems give a cost-effective way to the system or more improvements should be made. The assessment is in a bid to come up with a better word to define computer problems while maintaining the meaning but prevent final-users from denying the acknowledgment of mistakes.

Anti-Debugging

It encompasses the effectiveness of different techniques to stop the debugging process from happening. It is also the reverse engineering in computer codes. It is the contrary of debugging.

This series of events are commonly taken by developers, for instance, in the copy-protection plan as well as malware to notice and prevent debugging. Anti-debugging is the complete contrary of debugging tools which consist of protecting, detecting, and the removal of errors which seldom happen in Python programming. Below is a list of Anti-debugging conventional methods;

- Timing and latency.

- Modified code.

- API-based.

- Hardware and register-based.

- Exception-based.

Determining and penalizing debugger

Concepts of Python Debugging

<u>Current Line</u>

The current line is a conception where a computer can only do one thing at a given time, precisely, when creating programs. The continuity of codes is commonly controlled from one point to another by activities which only run on the current line to the other below the screen. During python programming, the current path can only be replaced by functions like loops, IF statements and calls among others. Moreover, it is not compulsory to start a programming code from the first line, but through the use of breakpoints, one can know where to start and where to avoid.

Breakpoints

Breakpoints are computing tools which alter debuggers in case of a problem and immediately stops the program execution and makes the necessary corrections. In a case where one is running a program in python package, the codes customary start writing from the first line and flow continuously until where there is a success or an error. However, if bugs occur either in a specific function or a section of the program, but the error codes may not have been used when input takes place. The error may persist not until the start of the program that you realize the problem. In these specific points, breakpoints become useful as they stop these events immediately. This concept, therefore, enables you to create a perfect python programming in just a short period.

Stepping

It is a concept that functions with debugging tools in ensuring that programs become more efficient. Python program stepping is the art of jumping from one to another to know whether program lines contain mistakes or errors which need correction before executing the program. Python program stepping occurs in three different ways step-ins, step over, and step out.

Step in: Step in function includes the termination of the next line in the system enabling the user to move directly into the coding and proceed to debug the supposed line.

Step over: In this stepping, the developer moves to the next line in the current function and debugs with a new code before running the program.

Step out: Step out includes jumping to the last line of the coded program and finishing the program before executing the plan.

Continuous Program Execution

Python programming may end up continuing a program executed by the computer itself in some cases. To proceed, command gives your computer the ability to return code input up to the end if there does not exist a breakpoint. The returning button may be different from one computer to another commonly because of the computer operating system and the type of language programming package. Python debugging has remained the most adaptable for different end-users and developers as there exist similarities between them.

Existing the Debugging Tool

The main reason for having a debugging tool is to spot and remove all errors in a programming function. After proper use of all debugging tools in detecting all malfunctions and problems within a program or codes, correction of the problem follows. The steps to follows start with fixing the problem by editing the characters, halt the debugging process, put a breakpoint, and start another debugging tool. Note, like in the case of continuous program execution the process may be different considering the OS and other packages other than Python.

Function Verification

It is always important to keep records of the condition of each code specifically when dealing with calculations and variables when writing a coding program. Also, the development of functions may stake up; this calls for a need for a function calling technique to know how any task impacts the other. Similarly, it is advisable to use the nested codes first if a step in is to be used to develop a sequential approach of executing the correct code first.

Processes of Debugging

Problem Reproduction

The main reason for a debugging tool is to detect any errors in a program and eradicate them from the programming process. The attempt to detect and reproduce either a new or existing error which is a nontrivial function or other unlikely software buds is the starting step in debugging. The method of debugging to be significantly used focuses on the current condition of your program and notes the bugs available at that time. The reproduction is affected by the computer usage history, current environment hence affecting the results

Simplification of the Problem

This refers to the reduction of the inputs of a program by breaking down the characters to a more straightforward elimination of bugs in the other process. In a case where large amounts of data are in a compiler containing bugs, it may crush during parsing as it includes all the data at once. However, the subdivision of files enables straightforward reproduction of errors hence preventing the collapse of the program. The developer hence identifies the bugs by checking unlike source files in the first test case to see whether if there are more errors which need immediate debugging.

Elimination of Bugs

After a successful reproduction of errors and the simplification of the code to check the bugs the next is using a debugger tool to know the condition of your software. Searching a well-organized and straightforward code allows you to know the origin of errors. Also, bug tracking can be used to trace the origin, making it essential to remove errors from the source. Tracking of bugs in python programming has a crucial role in placing variables in different places to have a high end of execution. The debugger, therefore, works on the bugs and keeps the program from all errors.

Debugging In Constant Variable Systems

Embedded systems vary when compared to the broader use of computer packages designs. They allow the users to have a number of platforms, for example, operating systems and CPU design followed by variant. They are made to do only one task to a particular software for the good of optimizing the program. A specific debugging tool is then needed to take a specific task which makes it hard to decide on one.

Due to its diversity, embedded debugging tools exist in different forms of debugging, for example, commercial and research tools which also have sub-division to specific errors. An excellent example of commercial debuggers is "green hill software" as there is "flock lab" for research debuggers. Embedded buds use a functionality approach which gathers the operating state information hence boosting the performance of the system.

Debugging Techniques

All language programming software uses a debugging style to optimize its bug spot-out and elimination; Python, like any other programming software, has the same. There are standard methods of debugging used, namely interactive, print, remote, postmortem, algorithm, and delta debugging. The approach used to eliminate bugs interprets the similarities between the various approaches. For example, monitoring, tracking bugs, and later printing them is done by print debugging.

Remote debugging is an approach of eliminating bugs which are running on a specific program but different from the burger tool. Postmortem debugging methods are to spot-out and remove bugs from already collapsed programs. Other techniques for python programming include staff squeezing etc.

Python Debugging Tools

Different developers have come up with various tools. As a result, users are found to be in a dilemma when choosing the best tool. Similarly, Python has a different tool that aims to help the programmer in debugging and have codes that are free from errors. Pythons' debuggers are also dependent on the operating system and its state; if it is inbuilt or acquired. As a result, Python programs debug based on the command line, analysis, or IDE depending on the available data to eradicate bugs.

Debuggers Tools

Python debuggers are dependant to the operating system. As a result, the two factors determine whether the debugger will work in a specialty or multipurpose nature. Examples of multipurpose python debuggers are pudb and Winpdb, Epdb2, epdb, JpyDbg, pydb, trepan2, and Pythonpydebug. On the other hand, all-purpose debugger includes PDB and PdbRcldea. On the other hand, specific debuggers are gdb, DDD, Xpdb, and HAP Python Remote Debugger. The mentioned tools can be used in different processes like installation, creation of a program, remote debugging, thread debugging, and graphics debugging.

INTEGRATED DEVELOPMENT ENVIRONMENT (IDE) Tools

The integrated development environment is ranked as the best python programming tool as it perfectly suits big projects. Despite the different tools in the (IDE), its properties remain the same for executing codes, analyzing variables, and creating breakpoints. The most popular (IDE) Python debugging tool is the Pycharm. It consists of full elemental operations like plugins for optimizing the performance of python programs. Examples of other (IDE)tools include; Komodo IDE, Thonny, PyScripter, Pydev, Visual studio code, and wing IDE, among others.

Special-Purpose Tools

Debugging tools required for detecting and removing bugs from various parts of the python program, mainly working in remote processes are referred to as special-purpose tools. They are more utilized in tracking errors in highly delicate and remote areas where it is almost impossible for other debuggers to access. Firepython used in Firefox as a python logger, manhole, PyConquer, Pyringe, icecream, Pysnooper, and hunter is some of the widely used special-purpose tools. The subdivision of debuggers allows developers to notice hidden and unrealized bugs and quickly eliminate them from the system.

Understanding Debugging and Python Programming

Before discussing more the relationship between the program and debugging, there are various ways on how the application conducts. One of the most significant components of debugging is that it runs code inside your program one at a time and ensures you view the process of data execution. They act as replays of what had occurred in the Python program. When the program is being executed, computers, provide less view, but debugger makes it possible. Therefore, python code behaves like slow speed graphics while knowing errors in the buds. The debugger enables you to;

- The flow of codes in the program

- Code looping

- Specific data contained in each variable within the program

- The addition, modification, and elimination of functions

- Any other types of calculations performed

- The techniques used to create variables

- How the ID and ELSE statements have been entered

Debugger Commands

Debugging is a popular feature in the programming language; a number of commands are used when maneuvering its actions.

The basic controls are the most important for beginners and may consist of abbreviation of one or more letters. A blank space is used to differentiate a command line while others are encrypted in brackets. Additionally, the syntax command prohibits the use of the square brackets to be written but otherwise separated by a vertical bar.

During inspections of python statements against errors, prefixes are added with an exclamation mark. This allows changes to be made to variables as well as function calls. A number of commands can also be inserted in the same line but separated by (';') with inputs spaced differently from other codes. In such cases debugging works with aliases enabling for adaptability between words in the same context. Aliases also maximize the need for reading files in the directory with faults though it is viewed correctly when used with debugger prompt.

Common Debugging Commands

Starting

The starting command is used in debugging 'start' to boot the debugger from its source. The process undertaken includes writing the title of the debugger, the name of the file, and the program to be executed. Within the debugging tool appears a prompt which gives one a number of commands from which to make necessary corrections.

Running

It facilitates execution of the command to the needed lines and detects any possible defects in the program. The command which is used is '[!]*statement*' '*run*'. The command prompt shows a number of arguments may be at the top of the package specifically when executing programs without debuggers

Breakpoints

As a crucial component in debugging, breakpoint uses the command 'break' [[*filename:*]*lineno/function[, condition]]*" to help debuggers stop code input process when program execution reaches this point. During programming, when a developer writes the values and comes along a breakpoint, the process stops for a while as the debugger command dialogue appears on the screen. This provides time to check on the variables while detecting any faults or problems which may impact the process. Breakpoints are, therefore, be placed to stop at any line either numerical or functional name which designates program execution.

Back Trace

Backtrace is an executive using the command 'bt' and consist of a list of all awaiting function calls to be added in the program the moment it stops. Backtrace commands can only perform when the execution is suspended in the breakpoints or after it has halt during a runtime error abnormally, in a condition called segmentation faults. In this type of debugging, conditions are more critical, especially during segmentation faults, where the source of errors are shown than the pending functional calls.

Printing

Printing a significant role in programming is to analyze the cost of variables or expressions which has been used in the function examination before execution. It uses the command 'where.' Additionally, like backtrace, it is only utilized after there has been a stop at the breakpoint or in cases of runtime error. The formal expression used in such an occasion is C possessing the power to handle legitimate C expression and also functional calls. Similarly, printing, resuming execution after a breakpoint or during runtime errors uses the command *'continue.'*

Single Step

The single-step uses the command 'step' 'next' after a breakpoint to step over through source lines one at a time. The two commands which are used to show varying indications with 'step' showing the execution of all the lines and the functions also while 'next' jump functional calls and does not cover each chain of the given work. It is important to execute the coded program line per line to acquire a perfect outcome when it is on tracking errors on executions.

Trace Search

By using the command 'up, down.' the coded program can function by either scrolling upwards or downwards using the trace search with pending calls. This type of debugging allows you to go through variables of different levels of calls on the list. That way, you can readily spot-out faults in the program and eliminate them using the desired python programming tool.

File Select

File select is another primary debugging command which utilizes '((list) *(first), last)).'* Some programs may contain more than one source files specifically with complex programming techniques, hence the need to use all debugging tools in such a case. Developers are urged to settle on the main source file for the ease in scheduling breakpoints and runtime errors to check the lines in the folders. When using the python programming language, files can be easily selected.

Help and Quit

The help command normally represented as '(help)' and quit, which is represented as '(quit)' both are of great help in program execution. Help command shows all the assistance information and can be directed to a specific solution to a current problem. The quit command is used for leaving or exiting the debugging tool.

Alias

The Alias command comprises of an alias word to execute a command, but the user has an option of choosing whether to enclose in either single or double quotes or not. The control used is *[alias [command]]*. Replaceable parameters go through indicators which can be replaced with other functions in the program. In such cases, the name remains the way it was only if the settings are left without commands or any question from the debugger tool. If so the alias may be damaged and accept any data collaborated in the PDB prompt.

Python Debugger

In python programming, the module *PDB typically* tells more about the interactive source code debugger hence, accepting to place parameters in breakpoints. It also gives a one-step impact at the original line level, listing the source code and analyzing the arbitraries codes in Python as a method of stacking a frame. Postmortem debugging is also held high under the title under program control. The source evaluation of *PDB obtained* shows how extensible python programming can be. The interface, therefore, uses *PDB and cmd* as and the other primary modules

The debugger command prompt *pdb* is important in running the codes in control of the debugging tools; for example, pdb.py invoked like a script to debug related forms. Furthermore, it can only be incorporated as an application to check collapsed programs while using a number of functions. Examples of the commands used are (*statement, [globals, [locals]]*) for the run python statements and runeval. There are also many more python programming functions which are not listed above to execute python programs perfectly.

Using Debugger Commands

As explained above, the debugger command wizard is a flowing process which shows a window where you feed your variables at the bottom. Outputs are shown, and then prompt is displayed only when commands are successful. The debugger command window is hence also known as the immediate debugger window. It shows two panes; small and the bottom one where you enter your commands as the larger upper one shows the results.

The command wizard is the window where one readily feeds the inputs to your debugging needs, specifically if required to check through your program for any faults. The prompt of Python debugging is user-friendly and contains all the relevant protective measure of detecting and eliminating any error. Therefore, the prompts display your current debugging command, and one can easily stop, change, or select any other debugging parameters.

Debugging Session

Using debugging in Python for computer language programming is usually a process with a lot of repetition, which includes the writing of codes and executing them. It does run not unless one implement the required debugging tools, check and correct all the faults, and then repeat the same process again and again. In that manner, the debugging sessions using the same python programming techniques repetitive process which includes writing codes and running it; it does not work, and you implement debugging tools and fix errors and redo the process once again and again. As such, the debugging session tends to utilize the same techniques, which hence demand some key points to note. The sequence below enhances your programming processes and minimizes the repeats witnessed during program development.

- Setting of breakpoints

- Running programs by the relevant debugging tools

- Check variable outcomes and compare with the existing function

- When all seems correct, you may either resume the program or wait for another breakpoint and repeat if need be

- When everything seems to go wrong, determine the source of the problem, alter the current line of codes and begin the process once more

Tips in Python Debugging

Create a Reliable Branch

The process of debugging is already proven to be repetitive, and due to the many programming language platforms, it varies; hence, it is advisable to choose one path. Keeping your own parameters has an important role in ensuring all your programs are coded within a certain environment. Therefore, beginners should ensure to set their parameters.

Install PDB++

If one is working with a Python programming language, it is crucial to install PDB++ software to help in maneuvering inside a certain command line. By the use of the software, one can readily access a specific prompt dialogue which is well colorized, and a great full tab showed smartly. A pd++ certainly improves the appearance of one's debugging tool bringing a newer and standard PDB.

Conduct Daily Practices

Continuous use of Python debugging tools is one easiest and fast method to learn and understand more in-depth about incorporating programs with debugging. One should, therefore, make a plan while using a debugger and try to create faults so that one may know what happens. Additionally, attempt to use commands such as breakpoints, help, and steps to learn more on

Python debugging came up with practical programs while greatly focusing on the use of debuggers to create effective programs and on corrections of sections with errors.

Learn To Work at Thing at a Time

Having an understanding of Python debugging techniques enhances one's ability to detect an error in a program but also the effectiveness of how to remove such errors. A perfect way to acquire such skills is by getting used to correcting one anomaly at a time, which is, removing one bug at a time. Start with the simplest errors and think before doing immediate correction as in some occasion may lead to the eradication of essential variables. Firstly, make the changes and test your result to know your programs answer.

Ask Question

If you may know any developer or programmer, who uses Python or other computing languages, it is highly recommended to ask them questions as they are greatly using this software. Also, social media platforms have provided platforms for many people to meet if one has no friend. On such platforms, it is good to ask questions on your Python debugging problems. One should also avoid making first judgments to any section of python programming.

Be Clever

When we create programs and avoids faults by use of debuggers, makes one feel excited and victorious because of the outcome. However, it is advisable to be smart with control to keep your head high and don't forget of your future plans. The success of creating a more realistic and useful program does not mean that you will always be victorious. As remaining in control will prepare you to use Python debugging tools wisely and claim your future accomplishments positively.

CHAPTER 4

COMPUTER DATA MANAGEMENT

In computer science, data is defined as the succession of signs which are assigned significance by how the computer explains them. Additionally, computer data can be described as all the vital information that is used to develop computer programs which are applied in different areas of the machinery. What should be noted, though, is that the definition of the concept of computer data depends on various elements which are decided by computer users and the data itself. Apart from the idea of computer data which has been elaborated above, there are also other expressions that are crucial within this field. These include digital, data about data and analogue information.

These concepts have various meanings. For example, metadata is used to give more information about other data. The digital data, on the other hand, implies the use of two numbers only to represent information. Analogue data is the opposite of digital data. Computer information is important to computers because it offers machines the rules to operate a specific task. These computer tasks are the ones known as programs. A program, on the other hand, is made up of particular rules that enable the computer to perform a task when executed. In this connection, the idea of computer information management and evaluation are essential factors in computer engineering. This section, therefore, is committed to expounding the different facets of machine information handling and the evaluation applied majorly by those who create computer programs.

Computer Data Management

In computer science, the concept of data management has different meanings depending on the area of computing where it's applied. The idea of computer data management is an essential discipline as information handling is an integral part of computing. This idea emerged in the 80s at the time when technology was picking. During that time, computer data management used to connote information keeping using disks. Because at that time, there used to be another field known as processing management, computer information management was not liked by a majority of people. However, due to the explosion of software usage in actual time over the past few years, data management has become an essential computing resource.

Definitions of Computer Data Management

The idea of data management has a variety of meanings as connected to the fields of information storage tools. One of the usual explanations of data management is that it is depicted as a part of the operating system that handles the tangible tools that are used to store information and improves its recovery on any relevant tool. In the field of file management, information management can be defined as the program that lets the user form, store, recover and manipulate data.

From the perspective of data administration, computer data management means the role that operates information in a systematic manner. This means that data management incorporates all aspects of information handling, tactics of assigning meanings to data and methods that users depict and recover information in institutions. The above explanations of computer information management share a common strand. This is due to the reality that information data management has to do with information handling and data recovery.

Modern Usage of Computer Data Management

Due to the current technological advancement, the word knowledge is stepping into shoes of the term data. This has had the impact of changing the phrase data management to knowledge or information management. This culture of replacing terminologies has occasioned disorder on how data should be developed and defined, which has led to the creation of the exact word. This term is known as big data which establishes the gathering and analysis of vast amounts of information. The phrase big data has enabled the development of Information Handling Centers to enhance the running of data by institutions.

Database

The database is information that has been systematically put together for easy keeping and recovery from systems using machines. There are two main kinds of datasets: simple and complex databases. The complex databases are modelled upon complicated designs and offer outstanding results. Computer databases are part of information management tactics. Therefore, database technologies contain programs which interact with people, software and themselves to capture and evaluate information. The database program has specific attributes that are relevant that are required in handling and administering dependable databases. Several databases combine to form a database system which will give rise to the database management system and all the relevant applications that go hand in hand with it.

Edgar F.Codd coined the concept of database management systems in 1970. His idea was that information must be retrieved as per the content. As several years have elapsed since then, there is a lot of transformation on databases which has given rise in their expansion, operation and capacity to manage information. Due to technological advancement, there is an improvement in database management procedures, particularly some aspects like processors, memory storage, and how machines network. These databases technological growth can be categorized under post-relational, relational and navigational as per information structure and model.

Navigational Database Management System

This kind of database management system was created in the 1960s. Through this system, the computer applied direct-access storage devices like disks. At that period, three central databases were created: CODASYL, Information Management System and B-tree. These databases were capable of scanning the data systematically, sail through sets of files and apply a fundamental key to enhance its function.

Relational Database Management System

This kind of database was introduced in the 1970s and sought to improve on the early development of the navigational database management system. Unlike the first system that handled a small amount of data, this system was able to work with massive databases and had an immediate search choice for the target information. Just like the navigational database system, the relational database management system was also impacted by Edgar Codd. His idea was that there was a need to do away with linked list storage and instead embrace the table format. This system applies tables which are able to separate information in normalized tables, introducing more storage space, putting in fresh data, rubbing and manipulation of data. The relational database management system has also done away with the reintroduction of links and pointers and is always up to date of the data within its structure.

Post-Rational Database Management System

This system came into being between the 70s and 80s. The aim of coming up with this system was to create a structure which was complex enough to handle both the hardware and software devices. During that time, it was felt that the first operations were sluggish, wasted space and were expensive. Due to the reasons mentioned above, engineers used an integrated methodology to form a database system which was robust and easily manipulated. Examples of such database systems include SQL, XML, system/38 etc.

Database Interaction

The information that is carried by databases is very vital in running of any institution. The databases act as devices that handle different forms of data. Therefore, the databases are categorized based on various parameters, including the kind of information they hold, application section, and other complex factors. Besides, databases can be classified according to the type of memory that they hold. In this connection, we have in-memory, cloud, active, information warehouse, deductive and others. As technology advances, more database systems are being developed with specific improvements. Grasping the various kinds of databases offers you a chance to understand the multiple types of data storage, information handling, and recovery of information.

Another important aspect of databases is the notion of interaction. The database management system enables people to interact with various databases. Additionally, through these interactions, the end-users can determine the models of the database system. These models include DDBMS, OOBMS and RBMS. The most critical aspects of database interaction are the storage, recovery and manipulation of data. Additionally, other essential elements of database interaction include application program and all the languages used. Computer technicians can additionally interact with databases when recovering information applied as functions of the software.

Structures of Database Management Systems

Hierarchical Structures

This form of database design looks like a tree or a computer folder. It has records that are linked to each other through a pre-definition in between the nodes. When an ender-use needs information, they go through a specific hierarchy and obtain the required information with established criteria. There are many downsides of this form of database structure; one of them being limited to its roles.

Network Structures

Although this form of the structure resembles that of hierarchical design, it does not comprise of a tree hierarchy and has multiple interlinked nodes. Due to this structure, it's easy to reach and recover information. One other strength of this structure is that it has improved safety attributes in comparison to the hierarchical database design.

Object-Oriented Databases

The information is this kind of design is perceived as objects interlinked in numerous nodes and is made of two to three objects. The design of this kind of database structure makes it the best in forming various functions when building a programming language. One of the benefits of this kind of arrangement is that every code, value, and character can be reached as the structure applies a robust operating program. Additionally, this structure is mostly used currently because of its high level of safety.

Storage of Data

The keeping of databases is made possible through the application of tangible material containers which is made of database structure and all the essential data such as metadata. This means that database containers enable the storage of both inside and outward information. There are specific database management systems that facilitate character encoding in addition to serializing of information and indexing. In this storage data, information is saved permanently. The aim of using materialized views and data replication in databases is to enhance a robust data management program. Through materialized views, data storage redundancy is improved for high-quality performance. The significance of replication is to improve information availability and running of many users and top-level perseverance.

CHAPTER 5

DATA MODELLING

Python utilizes software engineering technologies to form data designs significance for data systems used in particular official reserves. It quickly interprets and evaluates information needs within the parameters of the firm processes of the institution. This kind of data management tactic allows a professional modeller to work collaboratively with various businesses and other parties in the computing world. There are three primary forms of data modelling: conceptual, logical and physical designs.

Models of Data

Data modelling provides a structure for information which then offers a specific explanation and data shape in a particular information system. One of the reasons for using a particular form of a data model within specific systems is to attain compatibility. Additionally, using the same designs provides seamless information sharing systems, and exceptional tactics have the consequences of outstanding business support which offers more gains. In spite of these positives, data models pose certain difficulties. For an instant, some may have unknown properties and different data designs across systems. Additionally, data models may limit information sharing by online users.

Data Integration

Information integration is the mixing of data which is derived from various sources which allow end-users to view all the information at a go. This approach is essential for particular sectors, particularly businesses and scientific establishments, where end-users face vast amounts of data daily. This approach is particularly gaining popularity due to the need of various companies to work with many clients, other businesses and owners.

The concept of data integration was created in 1991 at the University of Minnesota, where a software known as Public Use Microdata Series was developed. Through the invention of this software, interoperation of computer systems was made possible by mixing different information within databases. Due to technological advancement in this area, the concept of data integration has gained a lot of popularity due to the development of robust programs that can handle big data.

Integrated Data Management

This computing device makes information handling easy and enhances its functioning. The device is made of combined and modular methods which are significant for business information handling and optimizing the data's operations. The main functions of this application are enhancing information recovery, improvement of speed, automation of tasks, ability to accommodate new developments, accessible of services, and simple to upgrade it. The integrated data management provides an essential function in managing machine information, specifically codes, values and other crucial aspects in programming.

Importance of Data Management

Data is an essential aspect of any corporation or business. Processed data enables enterprises and government to make informed decisions. Computer users rely on analyzed data to create software. These users also rely on data to conduct their everyday roles. Therefore, computer data handling plays a vital role as it provides the data needed for the day-to-day running of corporations. The core advantages of data management are:

- Enhances combining of a variety of data sets

- Improves the efficiency with which data is processed

- Assures steadfastness, integrity and validity of information

- gathers and compiles information standards

- offers safety and maintenance first-hand information

- Improves information accessibility and recovery by users

- Offers flexibility when collecting data for analysis

- Offers affordable expenses of gathering, keeping and management of data.

Computer Data Analysis

This is a tactic that is applied in computer science and entails data checking, cleaning, transformation and modelling. The main aim of subjecting data to the aforementioned procedures is to ensure that data is useful, has the ability to offer solutions, and can be applied in decision-making processes. There are various aspects of data analysis and methods, which are mainly used in specific areas such as enterprises and science. Due to the digitization of the world, the importance of data analysis cannot be gainsaid. Making an informed decision through data that has been analyzed is essential not only to businesses but to the scientific world as well. The significant aspects of data analysis include data mining, statistical application and business intelligence.

Phases of Data Analysis

Data Requirements

Before undertaking any data analysis, you must decide the features of the kind of data you require and specific needs of the information particularized. This demands that you must concentrate on the outcomes as well as the audiences that may require the results. It's important to equip yourself with information about the units that you want to study and the information that you want to analyze so that you apply the best data process that will ensure that you attain your objectives. There are also other factors that must be considered specifically whether the information is numerical or categorical.

Raw Data Collection

As per the needs of your project, you can obtain raw data from various sources. There are multiple experts that you should request for this data, such as analysts and custodians. You can also consult an IT expert in a specific institution to gain essential skills that will assist you in your data analysis exercise. It's crucial to apply relevant instruments when collecting this data. For instance, you can use satellite, recordings, downloads and any other appropriate tools that can assist you in gathering data.

Processing

After you have gathered your data from relevant sources, the next step entails data processing. You can prepare your data for processing using various approaches. For instance, you may consider generalizing your information or inserting it into rows and columns in tables. After doing this, you can use relevant computer software to process your data. For instance, you can use excel worksheets or SPSS.

Cleaning

After the acquisition of raw data and processing it, the next stage entails data cleaning. This procedure involves clearing any faults that may be on your data. These faults may make the results not to be reliable and therefore, must be removed from your data before analyzing it. The main intention of conducting data cleaning is to ensure that the data obtained is error-free. The mistakes that are usually found in raw data may include incomplete, duplicated information and data with errors. Through data cleaning, these errors are identified and removed from your data before analysis.

Different tasks are carried out during data cleaning procedure. These include: identification of duplicated information, looking for matching records, looking at inaccurate information and column categorization. There are various techniques that you can apply to identify these errors and delete them. You can use automated procedures, or you can seek the assistance of a user. For instance, you can compare the information downloaded from a site and the physically available information or any dependable source of that information. You can also conduct data cleaning following the type of data that you have. In this regard, there are mainly two types of data: quantitative and qualitative data. You conduct quantitative data cleaning to clear errors that have come as a result of inputting data with mistakes and checking any spelling mistakes that may have occurred as a result of mistyping information.

Analysis

Data is ready for analysis after clearing any errors from it. There are various kinds of analysis that you can apply. However, the type of analysis that you apply depends on the sort of data you have. For instance, we have exploratory data analysis techniques and descriptive techniques. The exploratory data technique, for instance, assists you to familiarize yourself with the kind of data you're dealing with. Through exploration technique, you can determine whether data requires more cleaning or is perfect.

When you want to understand your data well, you need to apply descriptive statistics comprising such entities like median, mean, node etc. You use visualization techniques to present your data in a graphical form. You can also apply various models or formulas to help you understand the relationships of multiple variables. In this regard, you may have such variations like causation and correlations. Therefore, it's essential to develop variables between data values and clearing mistakes.

Another design that you can apply in your data analysis is inferential statistics. This kind of analysis helps you to measure any connections that exist between different variables. For instance, you can apply regression analysis to determine whether if the reduction of publicity has an effect of sales and hence, profitability.

A data product is also an aspect of data analysis. A data product is a pre-installed computer program that concentrates on obtaining data inputs and providing results. This technique mainly depends on designs and procedures, but it can be an effective way of delivering information to consumers.

Reporting

After data analysis and measurements of results, the next important step is sharing information with the target audience. You can apply various methods to communicate results to the desirable audience. The feedback that you obtain from the market will assist you to figure out the next course of action. For instance, you may decide to apply the opinion of your audience, to conduct more data analysis to meet defined objectives. You can present your data analysis outcomes to the viewers through visualization techniques. These techniques are useful as they can elicit quick responses from your audiences. Through visualization techniques, you can apply graphs, charts and tables to present information. The kind of visualization technique that you refer will also depend on the type of data you're giving. Whereas tables are efficient in presenting numerical information, charts are useful in presenting quantitative data.

Analyzing Quantitative Data

Before you engage in analyzing quantitative data, it's essential to know what it is all about. In this connection, Jonathan Koomey explains some factors that you need to consider when handling quantitative analysis. These include:

- Inspecting and clearing mistakes of raw information before analyzing it

- Operating essential tasks for example column and raw data checking

- Ascertain min-totals and grand-totals of computations

- Verify the link between variables for example percentages

- Have the typical values to enable efficient comparisons

- Through factor analysis technique, simplify existing problems

All variables in quantitative data analysis must yield descriptive statistics such as percentages, and medians. You also need to analyze the distribution of essential factors to determine their closeness to the mean. You can also apply a method called MECE, which was invented by McKinsey. This design asserts that quantitative data issues should break down variables to their pure forms. The outcome components may further be split into subcomponents which will be exclusive and added to the early totals.

Certain cases demand that quantitative data analysis may apply hard statistical approaches to offer answers to specific analytical equations. These include such aspects as hypothesis testing, which will enable you to gauge the validity of a particular statement of the problem or whether the computation is true or false. The regression analysis is applied to measure how far the independent variable impacts on the dependent variable. One other statistical method entails the measurement of the necessary condition analysis. Through this method, an analyst is able to measure the advantages of allowance offered by an independent variable to a dependent variable.

Analyzing Qualitative Data

Computer-Assisted Qualitative Data Analysis (CAQDAS)

Presently, many researchers and programmers are embracing the use of computer-assisted qualitative data analysis programs which assists them to analyze information. This program more complex and comes with helpful highlights which are essential in offering useful and accurate outcomes. Additionally, this software is fast and provides critical knowledge of your information, especially the hidden one. The program has gained popularity since its inception and applied in different academic programs.

The program has been used in various fields, especially medicine, sociology, and education.

One example of a computer-assisted qualitative data program is MAXQDA. This software offers a more profound knowledge of data sets without any need for explanation. In this connection, researchers forecast the end-result of a particular analysis by concentrating only on the content. Furthermore, this software has high-quality instruments for sorting, changing, and analyzing vast amounts of information. Using MAXQDA, you can also investigate various kinds of data concurrently, which enhances data handling, explanation and analysis of outcomes.

Qualitative Data Analysis Software (QDA)

This software uses various data analysis approaches. It assists organizations and researchers in carrying out different aspects of their data analysis, including schematizing, discussions, theories and field studies. The qualitative data analysis software helps researchers who handle non-numerical information and need to avoid mistakes that may come as a result of using low-quality tactics. Additionally, the software can evaluate photos, audio-video information, and social media data. Furthermore, through this software, you can easily import data and apply it to the program for analysis.

CHAPTER 6

PYTHON INTERPRETERS

A python interpreter can be referred to as a bytecode interpreter or a typical machine resembling an ordinary computer. A computer program running written instructions inside a programming tool independently without a compiler compiling in a machine language is known as an interpreter. Python can either work directly using an interpreter or make use of a compiler. Python interpreter has three options to use for program execution that is source code, translating the source code, or running the stored codes that are translated by the compilers only.

The first phase of computer programming was done in 1952, which also marked the first use of an interpreter. At this time interpreters were similar to compilers and translated computer languages of low level which had been introduced into machines. Steve Russell introduced the first interpreter known as Lisp. He helped to create many more programs. Python's aspect is more advanced in features that are important to execute programs even though they are similar. Python interpreters can execute direct programs without requiring compilations, whereas compiles have to translate data first to form object codes to be able to execute easily.

How Python Interpreter Is Downloaded and Installed

Downloading and Installing

To download Python Interpreter, you first begin by visiting their homepage, www.python.org, to be able to access important information regarding the programming tool. On the left, you come across a list showing the different versions of Python to select from. Make sure you choose the latest release, which has many features and limited bugs. Python appears with different options of operating. Hence, you should click on a download that fits your OS.

Choosing a different OS can cause errors when installing or may fail to execute programs. When you finish downloading run through the file following instructions on how to install. You can either run it using default parameters that are set by the defaulters or configure your settings when installing. Depending on the operating system, Python interpreters have various installation procedures. For example, Linux and macOS have a pre-installed Python that only needs to be updated to run, whereas Windows OS requires downloading an installer before installation.

How to Run a Python Interpreter

Python Interpreter has various ways of running that is dependent on your operating system. Firstly, the program can be run on a desktop by clicking 'start' then choose Python to use as a tool while running. It will display some information before prompting you to insert the codes for executing a program. Alternatively clicking 'start' on your desktop, followed by programs, then Python (command line). After these commands, Python will begin to run just like the previous step without displaying changes in the dialogue. Finally, type the file name, and it automatically displays the Python file. At this point, the data runs interactively primarily dwelling on current information. Depending on the OS, the process may vary, but the steps are similar.

The Different types of Python Interpreters

CPython

CPython is known to support all the versions of Python, and their default type is a widely used interpreter by developers in the programming language of Python. 'C' in Python refers that CPython interpreter has a special function interface and other programming tools. CPython is also a compiler during the moment it translates Python codes into bytecodes just before interpretation takes place. The C extensions accept multiple compatibility activities even though it uses the Global Interpreter Lock that slows the synchronized Python thread in a given process. CPython allows programmers to use extension hence reaching a bigger population when the program is developed.

Jython

Jython is another version of Python interpreter that's found in Java Platforms supporting the first version of Python 1.1 to Python 2.7. It is referred to Jpython, and it converts Python codes to Java bytecodes hence making it useable to all machines that have JavaScript. It works with both dynamic and static compilers using all types of Java class that can be imported as Python modules. Apart from that, Jython creates an interface between current Java codebase and Python code, particularly when the modification has halted translation.

Stackless Python

Unlike the CPython that uses the 'C' factor, the Stackless Python lacks this call. It supports the Python to Python first version 3.7. Hence it does not rely on the 'C' to function even though it is present in the program. It also happens to be written using Python and 'C,' hence helping interactive channels, coroutines, task serialization, and taskelts and so many other functions. Python entails micro-threads used to prevent visual projections that are caused by specific OS threads.

IronPython

It is essential in the use of Python in the .NET field using both .NET libraries and Python. IronPython supports to the second version of 2.7 involving Python to the structure with the use of .NET functions. It can also be used to expose Python codes to other programming languages having the .NET framework. Main features of IronPython include support for compilers, equipped interactive console that is used to communicate between .NET objects and Python scripts. Additionally, IronPython has direct integration with Visual Studio IDE.

PyPy

PyPy Python interpreter supports Python 1.0 to Python 2.7 together with Python 3.5 to Python 3.6 and is also the fastest alternative. It is implemented and used in RPython, which is the only one used for statically typed programming. PyPy has multiple features that include JIT compiler, PyPy support C, and many more to give comprehensive compatibility just like CPython implementation. It also improves programming performance hence very useful for promoting the use of some Python codes. Its webpage indicates that PyPy is 4.4 times faster than CPython.

CHAPTER 7

PYTHON SEMANTICS

Python programming is one of the simple and highly advanced forms of software development. It comes with a simple to use and understand commands that can be easily implemented to fit any workplace. It can serve as a programming language in different dimensions. Since it is open-source, it can be used on different applications, including commercial applications. It is uniquely designed to make it easy for you to read and create a unique and easy to use code for all kinds of projects, both simple and advanced.

Python programming was developed in the 1980s by Guido Van Rossum with the aim of succeeding the ABC language inspired by SETL. In the late 1980s, it had greatly advanced, thanks to its designer Guido who had put on many efforts for its success in implementation. In 2018, Guido stepped down as the leader and developer of the software, but he still remained committed to see it flourish. With his contributions, he had earned a name, "Benevolent Dictator for life" from the Python community due to his excellent decision making and positive leadership influence. As of 2019, the python programming project is being monitored and developed by a 5-member steering council.

Python 2.0 was released on October 2000 with a number of great features such as the support system for Unicode and garbage collector that worked on predicting and detecting cycles. With more advancement and to make it even more powerful, December 2008 saw to the release of Python 3.0 whose features are used to support the 2.6 and 2.7 versions. It also translates Python 2 code to 3 partially. The more advanced features in version 3.7 and 3.8 are overwhelming.

Features and Philosophy of Python Programming

Python is a multi-faceted language that supports object-oriented and structured programming. Some of its features support functional and aspect-oriented programming. There are chances of its support using extensions.

Python incorporates dynamic counting and reference counting. In this case, dynamic counting means that Python does not have an idea of what the variable is until they run a code. It stores its contents mostly containing the value and the variable bound together into a memory container. On the other hand, the reference counting refers to the action taken by reference numbers, pointers, or handles to be stored in a memory, disk space, or an object as a resource.

Python uses a cycle-detecting garbage collector for all its storage needs. It is important for memory management as the contents of the memory can be retrieved anytime from computer memory. There are strategies at sight to advance the memory management option, for instance, the use of virtual storage techniques that helps in idealizing the available space for storage and existing resources. It ensures all applications do not use the same storage space and for security purposes.

Python's design supports functional programming in the Lisp tradition. It has filter, map and educe, dictionaries, generator expressions as well as list comprehensions. In functional Paradigm, it means programming does not involve statements rather declarations and expressions.

A function in programming language implies an element that is used to bind various statements and enable them to be used in a program without typing them again. In Python, a function refers to a group of similar codes and statements that work together to perform a similar task. They not only help to minimize repetition but also make the coded re-usable. A python's function is defined by '**def**' a keyword that represents the beginning of its function header.

Functions are categorized into 3:

- **Built-in functions** for example; help ( ) used for help and ( ) used for printing

- **User-defined functions** which give the user the freedom to use their program. It allows you to use the codes and re-use them anytime.

- **Anonymous functions**. These do not use the def keyword at the start rather use lambda.

Values can be used in a function through parameters. These mostly include zero or any other separated by commas. They are however optional, and they have a wide range of benefits including; clarifying codes, minimizing duplication, breaking down content, hiding content in code as well as recycling codes. In Python, the functions are flexible and can easily be changed.

Defining a function

Defining a function depends on the task it is required to do. It should be created in a unique way to give out the best results. For instance:

- Consider using the def keyword. You can then include the function name and the parenthesis. After the parenthesis, you can add the colon at the finish of the header.

- Ensure all the functions in the parenthesis are separated with commas

- You can give an explanation of what the function is there to do in the documentation string. This should be after the colon

- Consider writing the statements you need the function to handle

- The return statement is important as it allows the function to give a value. This happens after the docstring (documentation string) which completes the function.

Functions which are found inside other functions are referred to as nested or inner functions. Nested functions should not operate on their own as they will create errors within the code. On the other hand, inner functions can meet or access the outer functions but cannot be able to make changes to them. For the inner function to work effectively, the inner function should be considered and named.

Function expressions

Expressions are formed when operators and values are joined together to evaluate one value. Basically, an expression is anything that has value. Python expressions include:

Identifiers

These are used in identifying functions, variables, classes, modules, and other objects. In most cases, they are represented by letters from A to Z or an underscore (_) followed by a zero or characters and numeric values ranging from 1 to 9.

Literals

These are data that can be given to variables. For instance, when we say a = 10, it means that a is the variable and 10 is the literal.

There are a number of python literals types. They include the following:

String literals which can be single or multiline

Integers. For instance; a=10

List literals e.g. list= [1, 2, 3, 4 . . .]

Float literals. For example: a= 2.67

Complex literals e.g., 5 + 4d where d has a value

List literals e.g. list= [1, 2, 3, 4 . . .]

Tuples literals e.g. tuple= {1, 2, 3, 4}

Sets literals where set= (2, 4, 6, 8)

Dictionaries e.g., map= (one;'6', four '2')

Operators

Operators are known as unique and special symbols. For instance: & for and. They represent values which are known as operands. For example, you can use d' to represent 50 and 'c' to represent 20. In this case, d and c are operands. If you use them as [d − c], 50 − {minus} 5 = {equals} 5. 5 is the final value of the operation while − is the operator. The sequence a-b is a python expression since it contains operands and operators.

Examples of python operators

Arithmetic operators

Comparison operators

Logical; operators

Bitwise operators

Identity operators

Function arguments

Function arguments are referred to as the values to a function when calling it. Passing arguments to a function are optional, so a function may have several arguments passed or may not have any. Arguments can be passed either by position or by name.

Positional arguments will always be at the beginning list. They can also be passed as iterable (objects capable of returning its members each individually) values followed y an asterisk. For instance: age (5, 16) or age*(5, 16). 5 and 16 are positional arguments.

Keyword arguments possess an identifier before them in a function. They are also passed as a value-led by an asterisk, for example, cat marks average (male=36, female=45) or cat average marks** ('male':36, 'female':45). 36 and 45 are the arguments whereby either can come before the other.

A function can have a fixed or a variable number of arguments.

There are three forms of functions that take a variable number of arguments. These are;

Python default arguments

Using the assignment operator (=) can be used to provide a default value for an argument. For example, in the function we can use, msg = 'how are you today.' When referring to the function, if a message is not provided, then the default message will appear. If it's provided, then it overwrites the available default message. A function can have a number of arguments with default value as possible. However, when a default argument is provided, all the arguments that follow it must also have default values. All non-default arguments must come before default arguments.

Python keyword arguments [named arguments]

The values which can e used in calling a function are assigned to the arguments according to their positions. In Python, keywords arguments can be referred to as a function. When functions are called using keywords, the order/ position of the arguments sometimes vary. It's their names and not the position that matters most basically. However, when used together, positional arguments must start at the keyword arguments. Otherwise, the call /reference will result in an error.

Python arbitrary argument [variable-length arguments]

When you are not sure of how many functions will be used in the function, we can handle the issue by referring to the arbitrary number of arguments. We can use an asterisk in the definition before the parameter name for such an argument. For instance, *def greet (*names):* this function greets all the people in the tuple. [*name is a tuple with arguments]. The arguments wrapped in a tuple are passed into the function, and it's called with a number of arguments.

Calling a function

When you need to use a function, sometimes called to perform the defined task, you need to give a brief definition of what the function is supposed to handle when creating it. Once your program addresses a function, it transfers all its control to the function involved. If the function completes its function, returns its statement, the program control goes back to the main program. You ideally pass the parameters you need together with the function name and store the result received. In case of an inner/nested function, they are only called after the outer function has been called.

Some functions are also defined to call themselves. This Python is referred to as recursion.

The Zen of Python

The Zen of Python is a summary of the central philosophy of computer programming language. It consists of principles which can e used to come up with programs that can decide how re python programming language can e designed and created.

Here are the principles found in the Zen of Python.

- Explicit is better than implicit

- Beautiful is better than ugly

- The flat is better than nested

- The complex is better than complicated

- Sparse is better than dense

- The flat is better than nested

- Readability counts

- Although practically beats purity

- Errors should never pass silently

- Unless explicitly silenced

- In the face of ambiguity refuse the temptation to guess

- Although that way may not be obvious at first unless you are a Dutch

- Now is better than never

- Although never is often better than right now.

- If the implementation is hard to explain, it is a bad idea

- If the implementation is easy to tell it may be a good idea

- Namespaces are one honking great idea let's do more of those"

Python programming was designed uniquely designed in an extensible way while having the central storage for all its functions. With that said, it is easy and simple to add programs and values to existing computer applications. This is what led to the popularity of Python. Van Rossum created Python with the aim of creating a minimum central language that could hold a large library that could be interpreted and updated from different ABC programming approach that had a lot of challenges in the past.

Through Python programming, you will find it easy to create less complicated grammar and syntax and to give developers options on coding methods to choose from. It is in one of Zen's Python principles that there should be one way and preferably only one obvious way to do something that Python bases its philosophy ideology. One of the practitioners from Python Software Foundation authored a book that "describing something as clever was not received positively by the Python culture."

The significant aim of Python developers is to ensure the program is simple, exciting, and easy to understand y the people accessing it. The language's name is a reflection of its fun side. The name is a tribute to a particular British comedy named Monty Python. It is an exciting feature of the program to experience the techniques used in referencing materials and tutorials. This way, users can quickly understand how it functions and its application to computer programming.

In python programming, you will definitely hear of the pythonic. When a language or code in python programming is referred to as Pythonic, it means that it complies with Python's philosophy and its users can easily read and understand. Pythonists, Pythoneers, and Pythonistas are names given to the effective users or the admirers of Python. These people usually have more knowledge and experience in Python programming.

Python Syntax and Semantics

For python syntax, there are rules put forward to define and decide how a python program should be written as well as how the readers of the program and the computer system should interpret and make use of it. In most cases, it included English keywords which are easily understandable and simple to read, unlike other languages which use punctuations which might be a bit challenging. Some of these words include: def, return, yield, while, finally, import, right, while, except, continue, assert, and so on.

Indentation

Python incorporates the use of whitespace in indentation to limit locks in the statements. An increase in indentation comes after a number ion the statements. A decrease, on the other hand, signifies the semantic structure having been correctly visually represented.

CHAPTER 8

PYTHON DATA TYPES

Python data type helps in identifying the right variable. Python has a number of built-in data types that helps it function effectively. For instance:

Numeric

This is a data type that mostly holds numeric values. It is made up of four data types which include the following:

- Int- This form of numeric value holds integer values that are of unlimited length and signed. It may not be that challenging holding integers that are plain and are either positive or negative. It is quite standard holding plain integers that are either positive or negative.

- Float- mostly deals with precision numerical data that is floating and ensures they acquire their accuracy level of up to fifteen decimal places. They may represent the actual numeric value, but they are represented by adding a decimal point. The decimal points are usually used in dividing the number values into fraction parts. You can also identify the floating number by the decimal points.

- Long - this holds data of integers that are long and are popular with Python 2.x and 3.x. they may look the same as the plain integers, but they are all the time followed by the alphabetical letter "L."

- Complex- this mostly holds the complex of numeric numbers and figures. When using Python, there is a need to follow a specific formula to work out the complex numerical problems.

Python Boolean

Python Boolean is a type of data that holds only two numerical figures. The two values usually represent true or false, which is either logic or Boolean algebra. In most situations, the two values in Boolean algebra are mostly constant. Depending on how the Boolean affects or describes a condition, the conditional statements are linked to actions on how the programmer decides. In this, the value to be represented by logic does not necessarily have to be Boolean.

Python List

A list in programming refers to the form of a container in where all the structures of different data types can e stored one after the other. It is able to hold a large number of data following a particular order for the count. You will find the data in a list well organized in a sequence that meets the rules with zero always being at the top. You will find any data in the list in a particular place for easy access and credibility. Python list will ensure your data is preserved and organized in an accurate manner for better reiteration.

Creation of a Python List

A unique way of organizing and arranging your data in a list is through the use of inside square brackets. Creating a list may not be that challenging as creating a file does not require any builtoin functions. You may decide to have the same values for your list, but they will be stored in different places. You may need to have a good organization strategy that will help you create a perfect python list.

Adding Elements to a List adding elements on a python list may require a built-inn append function. When using the append, you can add a data element on your list at a time. For more data to e added to the list, you may need to consider using the loop and append at the same time. You can also add any existing element you need to the list using append. For better addition of the elements, you need to add them the end of the list, and it increases in number one by one for the append method.

There are cases where the programmer will need to add an element and move it to a preferred destination. In this case, using the insert method is mostly advised. The inset method may have a number of arguments to follow to make it possible. These are the value and position.

If what a programmer needs is to add the elements at the end of a list, you may need to use the extend method. It is most effective when adding values simultaneously. The number of extends will determine how long the list will be.

Accessing Elements from the Python's List

If you need to access elements in your python list, you need to consider the use of index Operator. It helps you access items from the list, which mostly is an integer. For the nested python lists, the nested indexing is the most used.

Removing Elements from the List

Removing an element from a list requires you to remove one item at a time. Using the built-in remove function, you will remove the element you least require from your list. If you need to remove a number of elements at once, you can consider the iterator method. If you need to remove and return the element at the same time, you can use the pop function. Removing elements from a certain position may require you to use the elements index number in terms of an argument using the pop method.

Slicing off a Python List

If a programmer needs certain specified elements in a list, using the slice operation method will give them the best results. In most cases, a colon is used in this method for instance: [: index] is used when you need to print your elements list which starts from a specified range,[index:]is used when the printing elements from a different index till the end, [start index: end index]is considered when printing elements that are within the same range and [:-index]can be used when printing elements from the end. If you need to print your data using the reverse order, you can use [::-1,]

Python Strings

Python strings refer to the organization and arrangement of elements in the form of symbols. Like in computers, which deal with binary and numbers and exclude characters. For a computer, it stores its data as o'sand1s. For a figure to e converted into a number, it has to go through the process known as encoding and decoding. Encoding is mostly used in the conversion process.

Creating a String in Python

When it comes to creating the python strings, there are a number of quotes used to enclose characters. You can use triple quotes when you are representing docstring and multiline strings.

Accessing Characters in a Python String

A python string can help you access the multiple and single characters. Indexing is mostly preferred when you need to have a look at the discrete characters while slicing can help you access a number of characters. Indexing starts from o and accessing a number of characters beyond that could lead to an index error. To avoid the errors, you should use he3 integer as an index. You can also have an option of accessing negative indexing for all your elements in an organization. This is possible as the last item on the string is represented y -1 and so on. For accessing multiple items in a string, you will need to use the colon function.

Changing or Deleting a Python String

Once you form a python string, it cannot be changed. However, there is a possibility of changing them by reassigning them with the same name. On the other hand, you can also not be able to delete the content once the string is created. What you need to try is removing the entire string by highlighting it and using the Del Keyword.

Operations of Python String

Python string is the commonest use form of data type in programming techniques. The string has a wide number of options to use in different operations.

Python string is among the commonly used form of data type. This is because; python programming can be able to perform a number of operations using the string. Once the programmer joins one or two strings, it is referred to as concatenation. Using the +operator, you will be able to perform this task in Python. When you need to repeat different strings several times, you may need to consider the operator method. If concatenating strings in different lines, you can use a parenthesis.

Iterating

This is one of the operations that can be done using the string. You can also use the string membership test in python programming. In this case, you should consider using the keyword "in" to examine the possibility of the existence of a substring within a string or not. You can find the python string in a number of **built-in functions**. The python string mostly handles tasks such as the enumerate function which helps return to an enumerate object and the lens functions which have the position and value of each time in the python string in pair form. The lens function, on the other hand, helps in returning all number characters to the string. It ensures the string goes back to its original length.

Python String Formatting

Using the escape sequence, you are able to group characters that have a varying meaning from the original and exact figures present in the string. It contains two or more character that helps a computer know what to do on a program or command using instructions. For a program to ignore the escape sequence, the r and R is placed at the very beginning of the string. The values and characters will show the string as raw, and any escape sequence should e avoided.

Common Python String Methods

There are a number of methods you can put in place when using the python string. Some of these methods include the lower, format, join, split, and replace.

Python Tuple

Python tuple is basically the objects or tools that are split using commas. It is immutable, and in most cases, it uses parentheses. You cannot easily change the contents of the tuple. It is easier dividing the elements that are separated y commas and parentheses in a python tuple, in other words, is written as ( ). When it comes to writing a value inside a tuple, you need to add a comma. 0 is one of the first indexes in the tuple.

If you need to access the data in tuples, square rackets are easily used in slicing the index. However, it is challenging to change or make adjustments in content in the tuple due to their immutable nature. The only thing you can do to change the value in the tuple is creating a new one using the existing content. You will also find it hard to delete the contents existing in the tuple unless you are willing to delete the entire tuple using the Del keyword.

Python Set

A python set is a form of data type that has no particular order. You cannot make any changes to it, and it does not come with duplicate elements. All the values in this set are unique, and they cannot be duplicated. You can easily remove or add contents to the python set. Considering mathematics operations, the symmetric difference can be handled using the python set.

When developing a python set, all the elements and contents of the set should e placed between curly brackets and a comma or set up a built-function to help separate the elements. It requires items that are unique, not of the same type. Creating an empty set does not need you having two clear braces but using the set( )function without including any argument. Indexing will not be effective in creating sets as the contents will not follow a particular order. It also does not support the use of slicing or indexing when accessing or need to change the contents. You can add elements to a single set by add( ) method. Additionally, for a number of sets, you need to use the update( )method.

If you need to eliminate contents from a set, you can use, Discard () and remove(). Discard is used to make the use of a non-existing element while removing the element will end in error. You can apply the pop () method when removing and returning an element. On the other hand, you can use the Clear() method when deleting the contents of your Python Set permanently.

Moreover, there is a new form of set, the frozen. They are not as easy when changing the contents of the set. It is an immutable form with similar features to the python set, but its elements are completely unchangeable.

Python Dictionary

A python dictionary is small in size compared to the normal dictionary. Its contents involve values and content that is not arranged in any particular order. However, it has a function that helps you identify a certain form of data you are looking for. All you need to create a python dictionary by adding items in between curly rackets while separating them using a comma.

Each piece of data is represented y a key which is unique and makes it different from each other. The built-in function can greatly help when creating a python dictionary.

If you need to access the content in the python dictionary, you may need to help your unique key which represents a different kind of content you may e looking for. Keys can w used in two ways: inside the rackets or together with( ) technique. Using the get method, you will get a none to respond wherever their key id no key found instead of key error respond.

Python dictionaries are changeable. You will not find it adding, changing, or accessing the content. You can update values and elements when you have an existing key. If your content does not have a key, you can add one in the python dictionary.

If you need to remove any contents from your dictionary, you can use the pop () method. The programmer will access the key and use it to remove the items, but the value will e replaced. Once you remove the item, the pop item () method will help restore it. In case there is a crucial error, for instance, your dictionary having no value or more than required, the clear () methods will clear al the contents of the dictionary. These contents ion as dictionary content could e similar to that of the list but all that differs is the use of the keys in the dictionary and the lost is identified through positions they hold.

You can develop a new dictionary y using the alterable Python through python compensation. You need to create expressions that have a key and a value using a statement that should be placed between two curly brackets.

Why learn Python Programming?

Python programming is a well-known computer programming language that is highly proffered due to its simple nature, positive results, and ease of use. Over the years, it has been recognized as an effective language that uses an easy to read coded data. Due to technological advancements and developments, it has been made easily accessible with improvements.

Here are the reasons to consider Python programming:

Better pay

Due to python programming high demand and effectiveness, python programmers are among the most paid among software engineers. If you need the best things in life, this is what you are looking for.

Well known

Recently, more schools across the world are offering python programming courses to meet market demand. It has been recognized in the past and awarded for having the highest number of users. You should not doubt its effectiveness as its authentic and popular among many. For instance, websites such as YouTube, Instagram, Dropbox, and Reddit rely on python programming.

Increased demand

Due to the technological advancements in the workplace, Python programmers are recently on-demand as more jobs yearn for their knowledge and skills in running their businesses. They are preferred for they can handle a multiple of programs at once.

Simple

Learning python programming should not be a daunting task even to a starter. With its simple to read and understand commands, you are sure to make the best out of it without worrying about complex features or advanced skills required in reading the content.

Multipurpose

It comes fully packaged with a free module and a library for easier development in web application and data analyzing. You do not have to learn it differently. Having all the knowledge is ideal as you will be more effective in your workplace fully prepared for any software development task. There are more resources t help you complete the most difficult and complex tasks.

CHAPTER 9

PYTHON MODULES

Python interpreter loses the functions and variables you had made when you quit and re-enter the application. It is, therefore, more likely, you are going to create a script when you are writing extended programs. This means putting into use a text editor for preparations on inputs and processing the file as an input. You might feel like dividing the program by coming up the several new files then can be managed easily. For that reason, python has built a module, a file that stores definitions and statements. You can describe a module as a library in which the code is stored. As a programmer, you can use this file to find code for using in your application. In Python programming language, a module is a file containing code. It allows the programmer to organize Python code flexibly and logically. A Python module is made up of correlated code grouped into a single one hence allowing more comfortable use and understanding. Python module can also be defined as an object having randomly named aspects in python. These features can be bound and referred easily. A module can also define variables, functions and classes. The code in the module is usually runnable to ensure language translation. Additionally, a module is also a software applied in programming to do specific tasks. For example, when creating a particular game, a single module can be used on the game as another one is applied when drawing up the game on the screen. Every module operates as a specific file that can only be edited or altered discretely. There are executable statements in every module that allow its initialization. One of the primary reasons models are used is that they help break down large programs into much smaller programs that can enhance proper organization and management.

Modules play an essential role in allowing the code to be used more than once. Modules enhance this process by enabling you to define an often-used function within a module and then importing it.

Several modules in the Python programming language are readily available via the Python Standard Library. This implies that the only single thing a programmer needs to install the module using a Python application. Other modules can be installed through the use of a Python's package manager. Similarly, it is also possible for a programmer to build their Python modules. This can be done because Python modules only need Python files with a .py extension.

Writing Modules in Python

In python, modules are in the form of Python files having an extension of .py. This module is usually named according to the name of the file. A python module consists of vast elements like classes and variables, given a definition and implemented. Writing a Python module file is just as easy as writing a Python file. The essential thing to comprehend is the definitions of classes, variables and functions that can be utilized efficiently in running other programs in python.

Loading the Module in a Python Code

To use the functionality of modules, it is essential to load it in the Python code form. There are two forms of statements that python provides. These are the from-import statement and the import statement. The paragraphs below define each statement.

The explanatory statement is used when importing the complete functionality of a particular module into another. In this situation, the feature from any source of python can be brought in in the form of a module to different Python file. A single importation statement can accelerate the importation of so many modules; however, irrespective of being imported to specific files in multiple times, a module can be loaded only once.

The form-import statement. In many occasions, a programmer doesn't need to import the module to the namespace. Python provides a flexible way in which a programmer can introduce specific elements of a module. The application of from-import statement does the flexibility. The statement proves to be essential when one particularly knows the elements that need to be imported from the module as early as possible. Code doesn't get heavier when the is applied. * is usually used when the entire elements of the module are being imported.

The crucial statements are used to access module files quickly. By so doing, an execution of the code module is created and definition scopes stored for use by the current files.

Whenever a module is loaded into a Python program, the following happens:

Python confirms that the importation process of the module is already done. If the task is accurately done, it comes up with a new reference and adds it to the existing module object or nothing is done at all.

Secondly, if it doesn't find the module the search for it is prompted. Typically, the search process is done by checking all directions and affirming by the use of specific file names. The file names used are extracted from the module's name that is being imported.

Upon locating the specific module name, python mounts it and then creates a module object that is later followed by a reference. On ordinary occasions, it is created using a specific module name or the name asked for previously.

Custom import name.

In Python programming language, a programmer is allowed to load Python modules using a name of their choice. Customizing a module is extensively crucial in scenarios where a programmer has set conditions to apply the particular the rest of the code. Customizing an essential name is made possible by overwriting the built-in import function.

Checking for and Installation of Modules.

Some modules are generally built within the Python Standard Library and give standard solutions. It provides the answers because of the modules contained in there that lay the foundation for the access of system functionality. Python standard library plays essential roles in the installation of every python. It's vital to click on the local Python 3 programming environment and set up the python interpreter in the programs command to ensure that the Python modules are ready for having. Operating the critical statement from the inside of an interpreter is also essential in providing that the selected module is prepared to be applied.

Renaming a Module

The flexibility given by python provides for the importation of modules given a particular name for the name to be applied in a Python source file. Renaming a module helps give it a name that is more meaningful or giving it a smaller name that can be used for many times. The keyword "as" is applied in renaming imported modules.

The dir(Modules play an essential role in allowing the code to be used more than once. Modules enhance this process by enabling you to define an often-used function within a module and then importing it.

Some modules in the Python programming language are readily available via the Python Standard Library. This implies that the only single thing a programmer needs to install the module using a Python application. Other modules can be installed through the use of a Python's package manager. Similarly, it is also possible for a programmer to build their Python modules. This can be done because Python modules only need Python files with a .py extension.

Writing Modules in Python.

In python, modules aRe in the form of Python files having an extension of .py. This module is usually named according to the name of the file. A python module consists of vast elements like function

Using the dir () function in python helps return a fixed list of names that had been earlier, defined in a passed module. The list comprises of sub-modules, variables and functions described in the Python module. The purpose is used in finding out every name is outlined in a particular module.

The reload () function enables a programmer to reload modules that are formerly imported through the re-execution of the high-level code. The calculation must be applied when reloading a module calculation.

Module Search Path

There are various cases in which a programmer needs their modules to be applied in different projects with varied physical locations. Python provides some options through which uses a module from a different directory is made even more accessible. When you search on a particular module, the previous search is done by the interpreter for inbuilt designs with a similar name.

Compiled Python Files

The Python programming language provides an option for enhancing the importation of modules procedure. This can be done by collecting a version of the entire modules into a cache by using a module. version.pyc, name. Through this method, a version of the file compiled is encoded and strictly uses the "a" form number from python. In scenarios where the compiled file is outdated, python confirms its date of modification and establishes a program to update it through recompilation. Every single module compiled puts into use its independent platform hence making it easier for a library to be used by files containing different elements. The procedure for collecting these files is an automatic process. It does not involve python modules nor programs automated procedures. Every single model maximizes its use on its independent platform, as explained earlier.

Scope of Variables

There are two types of scopes that are applied in python to give meaning to variables. One is that each variable is a module and usually have a global scope except when its definition is provided within a specific function. The second is that when the meaning of a variable is built within a function, it is regarded to hold some local scope with limits to its purpose. This implies that a local variable can't be accessed on a global range. In situations where two variables have the same name within various scopes, the local variable is often given the priority. In Python programming, the module-scoped variables are the single global variables present. There is no way of making a global variable. The only possible thing to do is making a variable achieve specific scope. The only thing that can be done in creating a module - global variable is allocating it to a particular name file.

Accessing Modules from other Directories.

It is important to note that a module build in python can also benefit other software programs. They should, therefore, be all designed in such a way that they can be applied in operating multiple programming projects. It is also important to avoid storing a module in ways that it can only be tied to the use of a particular programming project. In cases where a programmer needs to use a Python module from a different location from the location of the nuclear programs, various options direct them.

One of the choices is appending paths. In this option, a way that belongs to the module is invoked through the programming files that use the module. The procedure is considered a temporal one because it doesn't allow the rest of the system to be available to the module but can only be used during the development procedure. To apprehend the part of a module together with a particular programming file that requires a shorter process. The very first step is when the sys module, in collaboration with other modules that are key in the first program, are imported. The sys module is a critical element of Standard Library that is responsible for the provision of functions and parameters that programmers can use in their programs. The module can be used, for example, when setting a path that can aid the implementation of the identified module. Adding modules to the Python Path is another option that can be applied. In such a situation, a case module is added to the way through which python looks watches out for modules and packages. The solution is more beneficial because it is permanent and enables the availability of modules system. In this manner, the method of adding a module to the Python path is more portable, thus ensuring convenience. Operating the Python interpreter from a specific programming position allows you as a programmer, to quickly identify the way that python is checking. Each time a programmer decides to run a program, they should always ensure it is complete and doesn't contain any errors. Modifying a module's path provides that it can easily be found despite the directory a programmer is in. This, therefore, becomes useful in scenarios where a programmer is using a specific module to do multiple projects.

Cryptography Module

Coding in python needs high levels of interface and cryptography module to assume the role of providing necessary elements and recipes. There are specific commands through which the cryptography module can be applied. A particular code is also used in implementing the cryptography module. The code provides an output that is involved in verifying the module passport and creating a hash as well. There is logic included in the code used in the verification of the password and for the authentication purposes. The Hashlib package produced is applied for the storage of passwords in a database.

Generally, cryptography is defined as the process of communicating between two programmers through coded messages. In Python programming language, the major purpose of cryptography is to guarantee privacy and confidentiality in the communicated message among the involved parties. There are various terminologies applied in Cryptography. They include;

Plain Text: This refers to clear messages, and any user can easily comprehend it. It is the text that goes through cryptography.

Cipher Text: After the application of cryptography to a plain text, the result of it is a ciphertext.

Encryption: This is a process that a plain text is converted to a cipher text. The process can also be referred to as encoding.

Decryption: This refers to the process through which a cipher text is converted back into a plain text. Decoding is another term that can be used for the procedure.

Features of Modern Cryptography

Below are some of the essential characteristics of modern cryptography:

It uses mathematical algorithms to secure information. Two involved parties who want to ensure their messages need to achieve privacy.

It also operates on bit sequences.

Double Strength Encryption is a process of encrypting a text that was encrypted before for multiple times using a different pattern. There are different levels of double strength encryption. The first layer of encryption is when the text is transformed to become a cipher text. This is achieved through the use of algorithms and keys. Asymmetric keys then encrypt the symmetric keys. The second layer of encryption pertains adding another layer to the cipher message using a different algorithm. The third layer occurs when the message that had been encrypted before is delivered to the other party through an SSL/TLS. Hybrid cryptography is the processes where multiple ciphers are used together in various forms through adding advantages of the cipher. A basic approach is then followed in facilitating a random key then the encryption of key is archived through the asymmetric key cryptography.

Import Math Module

This is a built-in Python module that helps the interpreter in completing tasks. It doesn't give any feedback nor make returns to the prompt. This implies that using the math module doesn't need a programmer to do any program. The import math module is always standardized and readily available in python. It plays a critical role in enabling one to use mathematical functions under the math module freely.

In python, the math module can be defined as a standardized Python module that is readily available.

Math module in python can be described as a standardized Python module that is readily available. It is critical in allowing access to vital functions of the C library. Below are some of the function descriptions that accelerate the functioning of the Python math module.

Function ceil(x): Its primary purpose is returning the integer that appears to be the smallest but looks to be equal or greater than x.

Copying(x,y): The purpose of this function is returning x with the sign of y.

Fabs(x): This function returns the value that is absolute of x.

Factorial (x): It is used when returning the factorial of x.

Isinf(x): The function ensures that the response is True whenever x not considered a number or it's not infinity.

Isnan(x)This function usually returns True when x is a NaN.

Python DateTime module.

This is one of the most crucial modules that are applied in python. A DateTime class module is among the classes that are allocated clear decimation in date-time. Currently, the () method is used in the building of the DateTime object that often contains the current time and data in a specific location. When a programmer wants to create a current date, the today () method is applied. The class method enables one to create an exact present date to avoid common errors. Coming up with a date object is also made possible by using a timestamp. Unix timestamp is applied to mean the number of seconds with a specified date and January 1, 1970, at UTC.

Datetime.date Class

It is the date class in the DateTime module, where one builds update objects. The date objects, in this case, represent a particular date in the order; year, month and day. The function date()is the constructor applied in the date class. It takes the arguments year,month and day. The date object is used as the variable. It is only possible to import a date class when it is done from the modules.If a programmer wants to find the current date, the today () method is used. The class method assists in finding the exact present date and omit common mistakes. A timestamp can also create date objects. Unix timestamp provides the number of seconds within a given date and January 1, 1970, at UTC.

A from timestamp() method is used to find a date object by converting a timestamp. From this, it is easy to find the year, month and day of the week.

Datetime.time Class;

Its a feature of DateTime module used to create a time object which represents a current local time. Creation of a time object ensure printing of its components such as minutes and hours. It is the date class in the DateTime module where one builds up to date objects. The date objects, in this case, represent a particular date in the order; year, month and day. The function date()is the constructor applied in the date class. It takes the arguments year, month and day. The date object is used as the variable. It is only possible to import a date class when it is done from the module. If a programmer wants to find the current date, the today () method is used. The class method assists in finding the exact present date and omit common mistakes. A timestamp can also create date objects. Unix timestamp provides the number of seconds within a given date and January 1, 1970, at UTC.

A timestamp() method is used to find a date object by converting a timestamp. From this, it is easy to find the year, month and day of the week.

Datetime, DateTime Class;

The DateTime class constitute time and date objects. The DateTime constructor () allows for the appearance of the three original arguments which are a year, month and day. However, at the end year, month, hour, minute and timestamp are printed.

Example of a run program output;

Year=2019

Month=09

Day=12

Hour=20

Minute=57

Timestamp=1611913369.98766

Datetime.timedata class-in the time delta class; a time delta object works to show the variance in two dates or times.

Total-seconds method () is used to find a total number of seconds present in specific time delta.

The + operator is also applied in finding the sum of two times or dates. A time delta object can also be divided or multiplied by integers and floats.

Python Format in Datetime Module

Representation of time and date differ according to the rules of the organizations. The most common format used in the United Kingdom is date/month/year while in the United States is month/date/year. In python strftime() and strptime(), methods are used in finding time and date format.

Python strptime()-string to DateTime.

This format involves a DateTime object based on a particular string representing date and time. It applies two arguments in its working; by use of a string to represent time and date and also by formatting a code equal to the initial argument.

Python strftime()-datetime object to string. It is defined under date, DateTime and time classes. This method work with a string derived from a particular date, time and DateTime object. It uses a single or a variety of format codes which provide a result of the string formatted on its basis.

Handling Timezone in Python:

In most cases, programmers working on a project need yo display it in according to specific time and date of a particular timezone. The PytZ module is preferred since it can be used instead of handling the timezone personally. It ensures accuracy in calculations on cross-platform timezone and assists in solving ambiguous times' issues. The PytZ module is the simplest way of handling python time and date since it saves much time.

Difference between Python modules and packages:

They are both common ways used in the organization and structure of programming codebase. However, they differ in some ways; A python module is described as a file that has a python code while a package is a directory that contains modules and sub-packages. Therefore the main thing that differentiate them is the level of the file system.

They also differ in that a python package must have a file-init.p.y which are not found in python modules.A wild card is used in to import all elements in a module but not in python packages.

A python package can be described as a mechanism that improves the distribution of libraries; It helps in the organization of similar python modules.

Difference between python module and library:

A python module is different from a library in that a python library is a collaboration of set modules named with a similar name. Also, the python library differs from the python module in that it is a mixture of methods and functions that accredit a programmer to act on various programs omitting the code.

Python modules, on the other hand, include coded data in a python programming language. A library can, therefore, be described as the classifying of central python modules.

Popularity of python modules:

Modules written using python programming language are the most effective in that the process of constructing them is briefer. They are easy to construct since they involve finding a file that contains a unique python code and then naming it with a .py extension to the file. No sophisticated features are required in the creation of the module.

People who are interested in learning the creation of modules should take its benefits as a motivator. The benefits include more demand for software developers capable of creating modules. Python programming is mostly used by institutions and organizations worldwide. Some organizations work with large programs which need them to be compressed into simpler modules for easy classification and management. Thus they require programmers capable of creating modules to improve their programs.

Also, the use of python modules gives a better experience with python programming. A python programmer using python. Modules assist in improving the understanding of the working of every capacity module.

PYTHON MODULE EXAMPLE

Below is a written module which determine your age and if you are an adult or not;

#main.py we assume this is the name of the file consisting the code below,

def age(param): if param<18:

print('Not yet an adult')

else:

print('You are an adult')age (24)

When the function is called after passing 24 as the equation, it goes back to the following:

-You are an adult. This is because 24 is more than the known value, which is 18.

We are required to import the module first to use the code above as one by defining the filename with the module in an import statement as follows;

#!/usr/bin/python #import module main import main #importing modules.When this module is removed, it returns Not yet an adult, and this is so since the subject is less than the average age required.

CHAPTER 10

LIST OF TOP 10 PYTHON LIBRARIES

It is among the widely used and most popular computer programming language in this industry today. Python has a significant number of libraries hence simplifying the work when developing and designing of programs. Its other benefits include easiness and simplicity hence can be operated by beginners, productive, portable, and flexible, especially when compared with others like C++ and Java. Therefore, Python libraries have a primary benefit because only fewer lines can be written by the library leading to sophisticated levels. Advantages of accompanying Python has made developers expand their collection of the library.

TensorFlow

TensorFlow is a popular library in Python that was created by Google Brain Team. It is today used in almost all Google applications. It is mostly used to write new algorithms and building big and complex operations. It takes the form of a network to form computational graphs is several actions on Tenors. Characteristics features of TensorFlow library include flexibility, easy to learn, responsible construction on graphs, and a big group of programmers, open-source capabilities and enabling parallel neutral network. TensorFlow has also been used in Google Photos, Google Voice Search, and many more.

Numpy

In Python, Numpy is generally the most used library for machine learning by other libraries like TensorFlow that uses it internally to promote their performances. Some standard features of Numpy include easy to use and interactive, make complex mathematical algorithms easy, open-source contribution, and intuitive in simplifying codes. It can be used in many areas including threads, binary streams, and sound waves, expression of images and arrays of N-dimension numbers.

PyTorch

It's an important machine learning libraries that are used in hard situations like the creation of a complicated program that is used by developers. Some of these include hard computations with the growth of GPU, dynamic computational graphs, calculation of gradients. Alongside PyTorch goes with APIs essential to provide solutions to difficulties that arise from applications that are associated with neural networks. It is implemented in C. In 2017 a wrapper in Lua was introduced.

Features found in PyTorch include deeper integration with Python, hybrid front – end, comprehensive libraries and tools, optimized performance. PyTorch is used as an analysis tool for indirect language. A collaboration between Uber and Facebook was developed called Probabilistic library. Comparing

TensorFlow with PyTorch, PyTorch performs best and is more productive.

Theano

Theano Python library is used to calculate multidimensional arrays. It functions similarly with the TensorFlow but has some different performance because it doesn't have compatibility when it comes to environmental production. Theano features include when used with dynamic C code it evaluates expressions fast, great connection with Numpy, is capable of differentiating symbols, uses GPU transparently and stable and fast ready optimization. Theano library has been applied in handling unique network algorithms, and also it's important for beginners for creating softwares.

Pandas

Pandas python has a machine learning library called Pandas with structures of higher rank data together with their analysis tools. It can translate more sophisticated extensive functions when given commands by specific data. Pandas have many pre-installed ways to ensure it is effective enough to operate, including data combination, grouping filtering, and time series functions. The primary feature of Panda is focusing on the general of data movement in operations like sorting, aggregation, visualization, re-indexing iteration, and many more. Panda has had minimal releases, but in case of changes, it is updated in API, improving performance and fixing bug has been witnessed. In Python, Pandas are considered as great libraries when it comes to data analysis.

SciPy

SciPy is mainly used by engineers and developers. It's another library used by many machine learning languages. It's important to note that there is a difference between the SciPy stack and SciPy library even though they are both used by programming languages and Python. SciPy library has modules that are equipped with linear algebra, integration, and many more that enable programmers to design and develop new apps. Some features found in SciPy have originated from Numpy hence making use of it. However, SciPy has other features for efficiency in number routines, features like integration, optimization, and others as it uses sub modules for numerical values.

Scikit-Learn

Scikit-Learn is also a Python library, and it's associated with SciPy and Numpy. It is considered as one of the very best when it comes to dealing with complex data. The library keeps regularly changing, especially in the feature of cross-validation, giving its unique ability to use several metrics. Its other improvements are logistics regression that has undergone big modifications. Features of Scikit-Learn include cross-validation to ensure accuracy, neural network algorithms that are not supervised, and extracting various features from images. Therefore Scikit-Learn can be used to reduce dimensionalities, clustering data, classification, model selection, and many others.

LightGBM

LightGBM is a commonly used machine learning library and also considered among the best for developing new algorithms using the redefined models that are not complicated. These libraries are very important for designing fast and effective ways of programming in naming decision trees. Other libraries using the same approach include CatBoost and XGBoost used for solving reoccurring problems like LightGBM. Features in LightGBM include intuitive for user-friendliness, easy to learn for beginners, minimum errors, fast in performing calculations. LightGBM is scalable, productive, and well-optimized results hence boosting gradients of the desired outcome.

Eli5

Eli5 is different from most Python libraries because it is an in-built Python enhancing prevention of problems related to poor accuracy in model prediction. Eli5 has both visualizations and debuggers, giving the library a big chance to track, detect, and remove problems. This method of identifying and eliminating mistakes in algorithms steps has made Eli5 become one of the best of Python, reliable to determine the result. Features in Eli5 include compatibility with others like Sklearn-crfsuit, Scikit-

Learn, and XGBoost. The listed libraries can be used for different functions and give a more productive outcome.

Keras

Keras is also considered as a top and cool programming language library in Python. It provides a straightforward mechanism while expressing neural networks. Other benefits of Keras include a chance for compiling model's synchronization on graphs and much more. Keras also works with either TensorFlow or Theano, causing it to be slower compared to other machine learning libraries. Features of Keras include smooth running of both CPU and GPU, and it supports almost all neural network models, innovative and flexible.

Python Framework

Another name for the Python framework is Web framework. It's a collection of packages and modules used by developers to create soft wares and web applications without using sockets, threads, and protocols. Before the introduction of the Python framework, a great percentage used server-side technology. Introduction of AJAX code has changed this perspective with the development of programs being done with the user's browser. Therefore the web frame provides a conducive environment to create programs.

Developers normally focus on personal codes that have rules in the framework that are readily displayed before they write and execute a program. Hence these frames offer space for request interpretation, response production, data storage, and more. Of late there are many Python frameworks, but three standouts. They are categorized in;

- Full-stake frameworks

- Popular non-full-stake frameworks

- Non-full-stake frameworks

POPULAR FULL-STAKE FRAMEWORKS

Web2py

It is normally expressed using the Python programming language, and it is an open-source web application. It has inbuilt tools to be used during major functioning, and it's also a full stake framework. It was developed and released in September 2007 by Massimo Di Pierro allowing web developers to write web data while still using Python. Initially, the framework was used as a teaching tool before its modification. Components include HTTP requests, cookies and responses; several protocols like HTML/XML, CSV, RSS; CRUD API; internationalization assistance; disk and memory cache, RAM, and database abstraction.

Features found in Web2py include (IDE) Integrated Development Environment, portable cron, ticketing system, scheduler and bytecode capabilities of distribution. It first supported Python 2.6 and 2.7 and now a more improved and latest version of Python. All features are found within the package, so it is not dependent on other components found in Python. It also works with the following authentic systems that have libraries like ATOM, RTF, and AJAX.

CubicWeb

CubicWeb is licensed by LGPL and is written in Python language of machine learning. It was developed by Logilab and was first released on October 2001, and in October 2008 it became open free software. CubicWeb uses forge and Intranet applications which with time became commercial and leading used framework by 2012. Functions of this framework include supporting OWL/RDF, LDAP, SQL, and mercurial. Features include allowing for cubes library, tool migration, and selecting a view principle.

Being a semantic web application, CubicWeb has broader features, including smooth workflows, reusable components, numerous databases, and query languages. Its structure is data-driven making it function better, especially when the model is defined. Example of a cube forge is; It's important for a person to create his own and reuse it as messaging, comments, and file. It is hence becoming a great source that has originated from one framework. The components have been inbuilt, and on April 2011 it translated to other languages.

TurboGears

TurboGears is a full-stake framework of Python comprising of multiple WSGI components that include Genshi, WebOb, Repoze, among others. TurboGears structure was released in September 2005 having been developed by Mark Ramm and Kevin Dangoor. Its design resembles the architecture model view controller that looks like a Struts. Being a Python framework, it is set on top of middleware and libraries, and the series keeps changing regularly. Its components change depending on what is set on both, but they all have great benefits.

TurboGears 2.x has the following components Gearbox, ToscaWidgets, Repoze, Genshi, Ming, and SQLAchery. The previous versions TurboGear 2.3 was using Pylons as controller's repoze.what and Paster. TurboGears 1.x uses many features just like the present series, but it also differs in the improvements. These features include MochiKit, CherryPy, Genshi, Kid such as XHTML and SQLObject such as SQLAIchemy. Usability is either by app configuration within the given web browser or Genshi template plugins.

This chapter highlights the most popular Python frameworks that are used individually to accompany inbuilt components and also as web applications. This means there are many more other Python frameworks not listed in this article with limited use, some having been classified to be non-full stake and non-popular by developers. These kinds of frameworks include Pyramid,

169

BlueBream, Aquarium, Flask, Websauna, Grok, Pylons, Giotto, among many others. When compared to other frameworks, Python has proved to be the best using the popular full-stake frameworks.

Conclusion

Python forms a very integral part of society today. It is part of almost everything we do today. In this article, you got to learn more about Python. You learned about its origin and a brief history. You also saw how Python is being used in our day to day life through the subtopic applications of Python. Python remains relevant in today's world, and that isn't going to change anytime soon given the growing number of users Python is getting.

By the same Author

PYTHON PROGRAMMING LANGUAGE FOR BEGINNERS

A Crash Course Guide with Tricks and Tools for Your First Approach to Learn and Programming with Python

©2019

(Clark Wes)